A Tale of Acadie

by

Henry Wadsworth Longfellow

with Introduction by
C. Bruce Fergusson, MA, DPhil. (Oxon.)

NIMBUS PUBLISHING LIMITED

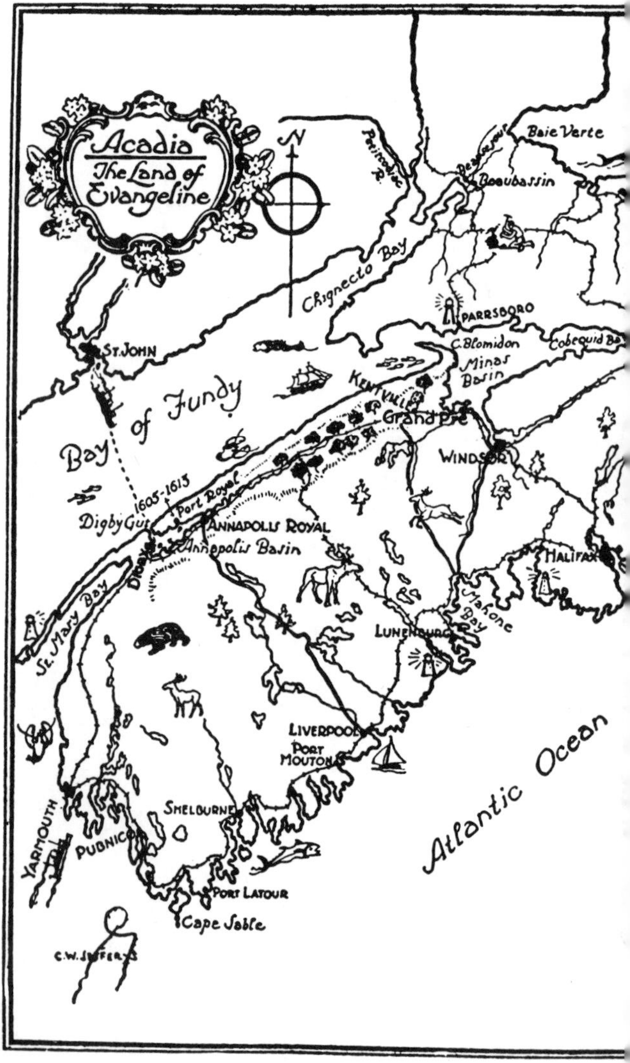
Acadia
The Land of Evangeline
N
Petitcodiac R.
Baie Verte
Beaubassin
Chignecto Bay
PARRSBORO
C. Blomidon
Minas Basin
ST. JOHN
Bay of Fundy
KENTVILLE
Grand Pré
WINDSOR
1605-1613
Port Royal
Digby Gut
ANNAPOLIS ROYAL
Annapolis Basin
DIGBY
St. Mary Bay
HALIFAX
Mahone Bay
LUNENBURG
LIVERPOOL
PORT MOUTON
Atlantic Ocean
SHELBURNE
YARMOUTH
PUBNICO
PORT LATOUR
Cape Sable
C.W. JEFFERYS

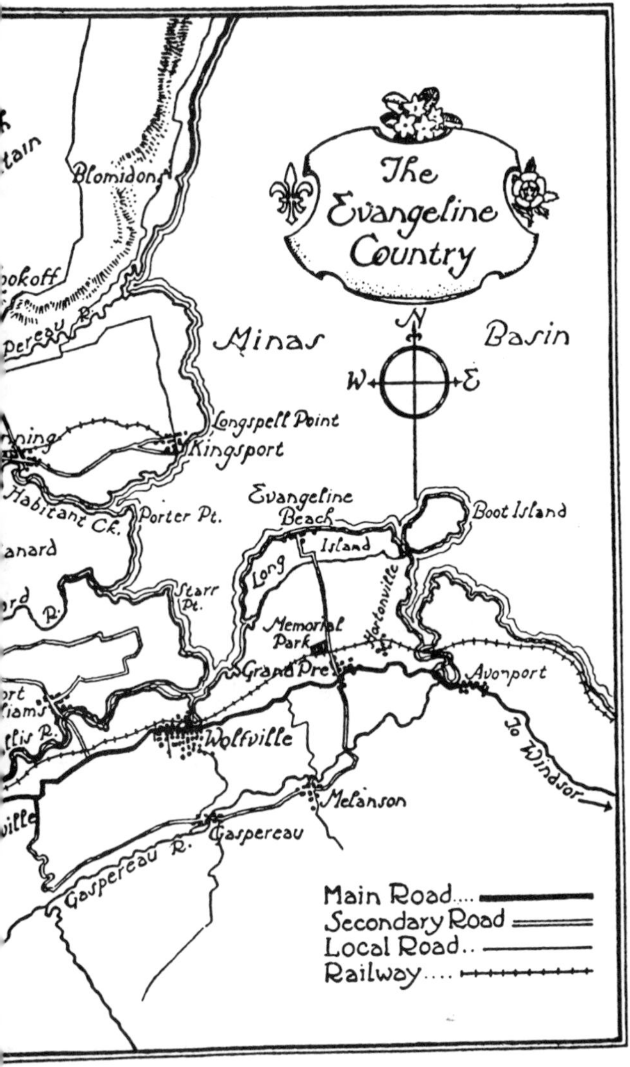

The Evangeline Country
Blomidon
Gaspereau R.
Minas
Basin
N
W
E
Longspell Point
Kingsport
Habitant Ck.
Porter Pt.
Evangeline Beach
Boot Island
Long Island
Hortonville
Starr Pt.
Memorial Park
Grand Pre
Avonport
Wolfville
To Windsor
Melanson
Gaspereau
Gaspereau R.
Main Road....
Secondary Road
Local Road..
Railway....

98 99 27 26 25

Nimbus Publishing Limited
PO Box 9301, Station A
Halifax, N.S. B3M 4J5
(902) 455-4286

Canadian Cataloguing in Publication Data

Longfellow, Henry Wadsworth, 1807-1882.

A tale of Acadie
Cover title: Evangeline.
ISBN 0-920852-13-0

I. Fergusson, Charles Bruce, 1911-1978. II. Title.
III. Title: Evangeline.

PS2263.A1 1982 811'.3 C82-007965-0

Introduction

Longfellow's *Evangeline,* one of the greatest of all the works of one of the best known of American poets, is, as it were, a work of art so charming in its way that its serenity and pathetic beauty shed an etherial radiance round the life of the Acadians, and lead us to desire to know more about the history of Acadia or Nova Scotia. It was published in 1847, ninety-two years after the culmination of *le grand dérangement,* and since that time it has run through many editions in the English language as well as many translations. It is still popular and, whether it is a masterpiece or not, possesses such qualities of melody and feeling, of pathos and simplicity, that seem to guarantee to it something like immortality.

Henry Wadsworth Longfellow was born at Portland, Maine, on 27 February 1807, and died at Cambridge, Massachusetts, on 24 March 1882. His boyhood was largely spent in his native town, whose lovely surroundings and quiet life he has depicted in his poem "My Lost Youth." At an early age he entered Bowdoin College at Brunswick, a town situated in a romantic setting, about 25 miles from Portland, and in a region filled with Indian legend. At the age of eighteen he was graduated with honours, standing fourth in a class of thirty-eight, which included Hawthorne, his life-long friend. Shortly after graduation he was offered a professorship of modern languages in his alma mater, and, in order to qualify himself for this appointment, spent the next three and a half years travelling in various European countries, learning languages, and absorbing something of the history and life of that continent. On his return to America in 1829, he entered upon his collegiate duties at Bowdoin College, where he remained for six years. He was married in 1831. Late in

1834 he was offered, and accepted, a professorship of modern languages and belles-lettres in Harvard College, Cambridge, Massachusetts; in the following year he made a second visit to Europe, during the course of which his wife died at Rotterdam; and in 1836 he returned to America and commenced work at Harvard. Meanwhile, as a student or a professor at Bowdoin College, he had written several poems and made a number of translations from the Spanish and French languages; and now amid congenial friends and pleasant surroundings at Cambridge, he continued to write as well as lecture. In 1842 he made another visit to Europe, and in the next year he married again. Eleven years later he resigned his professorship in order to devote himself exclusively to literature. In the year 1861 his activity was interrupted, and his life was saddened, by the outbreak of the civil war and by the tragic death of his wife. In 1868-69 he paid a last visit to Europe, and was everywhere received with honour. The last thirteen years of his life were passed chiefly in Cambridge. His courtesy and kindness were proverbial. He had a kind word for all and, though a great worker, found time, through ready sacrifice of his own time and effort, to dispense pleasure to thousands. His death evoked universal regret.

At the time of the first publication of Longfellow's *Evangeline,* the actual history of the deportation of the Acadians had scarcely been investigated, although Abbé Raynal had presented an emotional account of the Acadians in 1770, and Thomas Chandler Haliburton had used this in his *History of Nova Scotia* which was published at Halifax in 1829. Neither in the writings of Raynal nor in those of Haliburton, however, is there any story of the Acadian lovers separated at the time of the deportation and spending the remainder of their lives in search of each other. The genesis of Longfellow's narrative must therefore be sought elsewhere.

It appears that such a story did exist. It was known to a woman who married T. C. Haliburton's uncle and who later told it to Rev. Horace Lorenzo Conolly, the rector of St. Matthew's Episcopal Church in South Boston. Conolly related it to Nathaniel Hawthorne who, on 24 October 1838, jotted down in his note-book that Conolly "heard from a French Canadian the story of a young couple in Acadia":

"On their marriage day, all the men of the Province were summoned to assemble in the church to hear a proclamation. When assembled, they were all seized and shipped off to be distributed through New England, — among them the new bridegroom. His bride set off in search of him, — wandered about New England all her lifetime, and at last, when she was old, she found her bridegroom on his death-bed. The shock was so great that it killed her likewise."

A year or two later, when Hawthorne went to dine with his friend at Cambridge, and took the Rev. Mr. Conolly with him, Longfellow heard this story from the clergyman. Longfellow followed Conolly's narrative with rapt attention and deep interest, and at its conclusion is reported to have said: "It is the best illustration of faithfulness and the constancy of woman that I have ever heard or read." He wondered why this legend did not strike the fancy of Hawthorne, and asked the latter to give it to him for a poem. To that request Hawthorne assented, and promised not to treat the subject in prose until Longfellow had tried to deal with it in verse.

In 1841 Longfellow was no doubt spurred on to carry out his purpose by the appearance of two articles regarding the eviction of the Acadians. One was the account of "The Removal of the Inhabitants of Acadia," which Hawthorne included in a little book called *Famous Old People,* and which he sent to Longfellow. The other, which was entitled, "The Exiles of Acadia," and written by the historian George Bancroft, appeared, along with some verses of Longfellow, in the volume *The Token*. Another publication of 1841 which has been claimed as suggesting to Longfellow the story of *Evangeline* was a novel by Mrs. Catherine Arnold Williams entitled *The Neutral French,* or *The Exiles of Nova Scotia.* But the story of the novel is very different from that of the poem, and such superficial resemblances as do exist are probably due to the fact that both used the same sources. Moreover, Longfellow had his story well in mind before 1841; twelve years later he declared that *Evangeline* had been suggested not by *The Neutral French* but, in its bare outline, by a friend of Hawthorne; and, on another occasion, he said: "The authorities I mostly relied on in writing *Evangeline* were the Abbé Raynal and Mr. Haliburton: the first for the pastoral, simple life of the Acadians; the second for the history of their banishment." It has also been suggested that Longfellow may have consulted in its original manuscript form "The Journal of Colonel John Winslow of the Provincial Troops, while engaged in removing the Acadian French Inhabitants from Grand Pré, and the neighbouring settlements in the Autumn of the year 1755," which was kept in the Library of the Massachusetts Historical Society. At any rate it is known that on 3 March 1841 he borrowed from the Harvard College Library both volumes of Haliburton's *History of Nova Scotia,* which gave him the background of the history of the banishment of the Acadians, against which he could set the legend of the Acadian lovers.

Yet it was not until 28 November 1845 that Longfellow was free to begin the manuscript of *Evangeline, A Tale of Acadie,* and not until two years later that this memorable work was published.

The first part of the poem, whose opening words "This is the forest primeval" are said to be as familiar as "Arma virumque cano," the opening words of Virgil's *Aeneid,* mirrors Raynal's view of Acadian life before the banishment as an Arcadian and idyllic existence, and reflects the impressions Longfellow had gathered from his travels in Sweden and his translations from the Swedish and the German. Longfellow had not only translated works of the Swedish poet Tegnér and Goethe's *Hermann und Dorothea* but had also published in 1841 an article entitled "Life in Sweden," depicting the peaceful life he had found among the Swedish peasants; and this description seems to have supplied some of the colour which he gave to the picture of the Acadian peasants in the opening cantos of *Evangeline.* Though the story in *Hermann und Dorothea* differs from that of *Evangeline,* much of the atmosphere of simplicity and the tragedy of exile are similar, so that Oliver Wendell Holmes may have some justification for his remark that Dorothea was the mother of Evangeline. It is also likely that the use of hexameters by Tegnér and Goethe encouraged Longfellow to use in Evangeline that metre which is as "musical as is Apollo's lute." His manuscript and journal both indicate some uncertainty with respect to the names to be given to such characters as Evangeline herself, Gabriel, Basil the blacksmith and the priest. The first part of the poem has its scene the Acadian village of Grand Pré, which Longfellow never saw, and contains bits of French folklore, which the poet read in Pluquet's *Contes Populaire,* as well as songs from *Receuil de Cantiques, à l'usage des Missions, Retraites et Catechismes,* which was published at Quebec in 1833.

In the second part of the poem Longfellow unfolded the extensive panorama of the whole continent, although he himself had seen neither the Mississippi,

Louisiana nor the West. As a boy of nineteen, however, he had visited Philadelphia, and seen the old Alms House, which he had in mind as the place of the last meeting of Evangeline and Gabriel. There he had also seen "an old Catholic grave-yard not far away" and there, "in the heart of the city," he afterwards imagined Evangeline and Gabriel "lying buried and unnoticed." In Watson's *Annals of Philadelphia* he read about the yellow fever there in 1793, and he apparently decided to portray Gabriel, nearly forty years after his banishment from Nova Scotia, dying as one of the many pitiful victims of that epidemic. As preparation for that part of the poem which deals with Evangeline's voyage down the Ohio to the Mississippi and to the Bayous of Louisiana, Longfellow read the description written by his sister of her voyage down the Ohio and Mississippi to New Orleans, and several travel books, as well as Audubon's *Ornithological Biography,* and saw Bonvard's *"Diorama of the Mississippi."* Information for his description of the West was gleaned from accounts of expeditions, travel books and books about Indians as well as maps, and Kip's *Early Jesuit Missions in North America.* Thus Longfellow saw even American life largely through his library, and the Evangeline of the poem is taken by the writer far beyond the territories of the Acadian bride in Connolly's story, who had "wandered about New England all her lifetime."

It is clear that Longfellow, when he wrote *Evangeline,* was writing neither a history nor a book of travels, yet its almost majestic serenity, its pathetic beauty, its deep sensibility, its slow melody and its reflective emotion have fascinated its readers and touched and improved the hearts of thousands upon thousands. "I have read it," Hawthorne declared, "with more pleasure than it would be decorous to express." It has been described as a mixture of the artificial and the natural, or as a work of art which we regard without thinking of all its characters as if they lived in the very next street. There may be no passion in it; its love scenes may lack warmth; but they have delicate beauty; and throughout the poem there is a sweet and limpid purity, and a perpetual air of youth and innocence and tenderness. Longfellow's view of the world was essentially religious and subjective, and his manner of dealing with it hymnal or lyric. He had a special fondness for accounts of human devotion and self-sacrifice, whether found in legends, tales, sagas or bits of American history. These traits of Longfellow are displayed in *Evangeline,* a poem which turns our thoughts to the story of Acadia and the Acadians, and the history of Nova Scotia.

The word Acadia was first used by the French to distinguish the maritime part of New France from the western part. The territory to which it was applied, although the boundaries were never clearly defined, and eventually became a cause of war between French and English, comprised what are today the provinces of Nova Scotia, New Brunswick and Prince Edward Island, and parts of Quebec and Maine. It was not until 1604-1605 that the first real attempt at settlement was made in this region, although Cabot had probably reached Cape Breton in 1497, and Cartier landed on Prince Edward Island in 1534, and abortive attempts at settlement had been made at Sable Island by Baron de Léry in 1518 and Marquis de la Roche in 1598.

DeMonts, who gathered his colonists, equipped his two ships and set out from Havre de Grace in April 1604, had been granted vice-regal powers as well as a trading monopoly for ten years. His expedition was a goodly company of about 150 Frenchmen, comprising convicts, labourers and artisans, fishermen, soldiers and clergymen, both Roman Catholic and Huguenot, and some gentlemen of noble birth, including Jean de

Biencourt, Baron de Poutrincourt, and the explorer Champlain. De Monts himself was interested primarily in furs, fish and minerals, while Champlain himself stated that the settlement of Acadia was secondary to the discovery and control of a passage to the east, and that the cost of exploration and settlement was to be met by the monopoly of the fur-trade. Be that as it may, however, Cape La Héve, on the south-eastern coast of Nova Scotia, was reached in May, and after sailing round Cape Sable and up the Bay of Fundy the newcomers entered Annapolis Basin, which Champlain called Port Royal. Poutrincourt was so attracted by Port Royal and its environs that he sought and obtained from De Monts this place as an estate for his family, and thus became the seigneur of Port Royal. Turning their vessel westward these Frenchmen passed the mouth of the river St. John, and sailed on to Passamaquoddy Bay. There De Monts landed his colonists on Dochet Island, near the mouth of the river St. Croix. There they built their Habitation de l'Isle Sainte-Croix, and there, after the vessels unfurled their sails and departed for France, seventy-nine remained to face the winter in the new world. By spring, however, thirty-five of the company had died of scurvy, twenty more narrowly escaped the same fate and, in June, after the arrival of a vessel bringing supplies from France, De Monts and Champlain set out from this island, whose soil was sandy and which possessed no fresh water, in search of a better site. They went southward along the coast, and established friendly contacts with a number of Indian tribes, but ran into difficulties with the Indians near Cape Cod, failed to find any passage to the east, and found no site which they deemed suitable for a settlement. Accordingly they decided to tempt fate at Poutrincourt's estate at Port Royal, and in August the colonists moved across the Bay of Fundy, and landed on the north side of the Annapolis Basin. Thus was founded in 1605 the first agricultural settlement of Europeans on soil which is now Canadian.

Other beginnings were also made at Port Royal. The Order of Good Cheer was founded in which all could vie in the preparation of entertainment and in the maintenance of morale. Thither in 1606 came Lescarbot, chronicler, lawyer and farmer, who wrote at Port Royal *The Theatre of Neptune,* a playlet which was performed there in 1606. Poutrincourt, and Lescarbot, and Louis Hébert, who afterwards became the first tiller of the soil at Quebec, engaged in agricultural experiments. And thither in 1611 came the Jesuits Biard and Massé, the first of the black-robed followers of Loyola to reach New France.

Meanwhile, owing to intrigues at the French court, De Monts lost his charter in 1607, Port Royal was temporarily abandoned by the French, and Membertou, sagamore of the Micmacs, 'a man of a hundred summers' and 'the most formidable savage within the memory of man,' and his tribe were left as the possessors of Acadia. Three years later, however, Poutrincourt and his son, Charles de Biencourt, re-established the colony at Port Royal.

But soon again the story was interrupted. A reflection of the religious conflict at home appeared in the colony with the result that the Jesuit party in 1613 decided to establish a colony of its own at Mount Desert on the coast of Maine, and that decision led to the destruction of Port Royal by the English of Virginia under Samuel Argall. This international rivalry might have been foreshadowed earlier, for the grant to De Monts in 1603 of all lands lying between the fortieth and forty-sixth degrees of north latitude had been followed closely in England by a charter granting to the London and Plymouth companies all the territories between the thirty-fourth and forty-fifth parallels, then known as Virginia. This region therefore not only included both

St. Croix and Port Royal, but also provided a basis for future rivalry for control of the Indians and the fur-trade. Moreover, when the English of Virginia heard the news that the French king had made a grant of all the lands on the Atlantic coast from the St. Lawrence to Florida, Argall was commissioned as Admiral of Virginia in 1612, and instructed not only to continue fishing operations but also, when occasion arose, to expel interlopers from the territories of Virginia. The upshot was that in 1613 Argall both frustrated the French attempt at Mount Desert and destroyed the French colony at Port Royal. Now the only Frenchmen in Acadia were Biencourt and a mere handful of companions who were to wander homeless among the Indians until Biencourt established his headquarters in the Cape Sable district. On his death in 1623 he bequeated his rights in Acadia to his friend and companion, Charles de la Tour.

Twenty years elapsed before the French made another organized effort to colonize Acadia. During that interval, however, while French missionaries from Quebec took up their abode among the Indians in what is now New Brunswick, the English founded Plymouth, Salem and Boston, and Sir William Alexander was granted New Scotland, and made several efforts at colonization, which culminated in the establishment of the Scots Fort, near the abandoned site of Port Royal, and a short-lived settlement at Baleine in Cape Breton Island. By the Treaty of St. Germain-en-Laye, however, in 1632, Port Royal was returned to France in return for the unpaid dowry of Queen Henrietta Maria. An interesting development of this period was the beginning of a dual allegiance on the part of the La Tours, Claude the father, and Charles the son. On hearing of the organization of the Company of New France in 1627, the elder La Tour went to France to procure supplies and ammunition, and to petition the king for authority for his son to defend Acadia against the English. While returning to Acadia in 1628, Claude was taken prisoner by the Kirkes, and carried to England. There he entered into alliance with the English, accepted grants of land from Sir William Alexander, had himself and his son made Baronets of Nova Scotia, and promised to have his son brought over to the side of the English. When Claude returned, however, his son apparently accepted the patent but refused to change his allegiance at that time, and in 1631 received a commission from the French king as lieutenant-general of Acadia. Later Charles's patent from the English king was used to advantage by the younger La Tour.

Between 1627, when the Company of New France was organized, and 1632, when Acadia was restored to France, Richelieu's colonization project was interrupted by the activity of the Kirkes, but in the latter year Isaac de Razilly was commissioned to receive Acadia from the Scots, and appointed lieutenant-general of the colony. He brought out with him three hundred settlers, who were mainly recruited in Touraine and Britanny. These formed the first considerable body of permanent settlers in Acadia. Razilly established himself at La Héve; but after his death in 1635, his cousin, companion and successor, Charles de Menou, Sieur d'Aulnay Charnisay, took up his headquarters at Port Royal, about six miles further up the river than the original Port Royal, and on the opposite side of the river.

Between 1632 and 1654 the French were left in undisturbed possession of Acadia by the English, yet the colony was riven by the struggle for supremacy on the part of the rival French leaders. La Tour, whose commission granting him authority over the whole of Acadia had apparently never been rescinded, had established himself at the mouth of the St. John River.

He disputed with Charnisay the control of Acadia, and not even the decision of the king of France to divide the territory between them was sufficient to prevent the rivalry from developing into open warfare. In the struggle for mastery it seemed that the laurels were all to go to Charnisay, when in 1645 La Tour's Fort St. John was captured, despite the heroic resistance of Madame La Tour, in the absence of her husband, and La Tour himself was impoverished and driven into exile. But Charnisay's victory was of short duration, for his death occurred in 1650, and in the following year La Tour returned to Acadia. He consolidated his position in the colony by means of a new patent from the king, making him governor and lieutenant-general of Acadia, and by marrying the widow of his old rival Charnisay. The strife in the colony was not yet over, however, for Charnisay's creditor, Le Borgne, claiming his debtor's entire estate, now endeavoured to evict both La Tour and Nicolas Denys, who was engaged in fishing operations along the coast of Acadia. This struggle was brought to an abrupt end in 1654 when the country again fell to the English. La Tour now put to good use his patent from the English king. His claims were recognized, and he was permitted to retain his post at the St. John River, where he remained until his death in 1666.

Meanwhile, although the development of the colony was hampered by internal strife, several small accessions were made to the population. Between 1639 and 1649 Charnisay brought out a number of French immigrants, and in 1651 a few others accompanied La Tour on his return to the colony. After his second marriage, moreover, La Tour had five children, who married and settled in Acadia.

From 1654 to 1667 the English were in nominal control of the colony and, though it was restored to France by the Treaty of Breda in the latter year, its posts were only finally, and reluctantly, given up to the French by Sir Thomas Temple in 1670.

The last forty years of French control in Acadia, from 1670 to 1710, included a period of slow, peaceful development, followed by one marked by raids and international strife. These years ended with the final capture of Port Royal, and its transition to Annapolis Royal, the capital of Nova Scotia.

Some development is indicated by the increase in population. In 1671 the population, which numbered about 400, apart from officials and soldiers, received an addition from France of fifty-five men and five women or girls. Thus these were added to the La Tour family, the 300 immigrants brought out by Razilly, the few additional settlers brought out under the auspices of Charnisay or accompanying La Tour in 1651, and the occasional soldier or fisherman who chose to remain in the colony, to form ancestors of the Acadian people. By 1710 the population had risen to nearly 2,100, chiefly in the districts of Port Royal, Minas, and Chignecto.

These people were a close-knit, homogeneous and almost self-sufficient colony. On the whole they were happy, healthy and virtuous, attached to their religion and their traditions, influenced by their environment, and almost independent of the outside world; notwithstanding the bulk of the direct descriptions of these people, which are of the mid-eighteenth century or later, and which are from accounts of soldiers little in sympathy with them, or by others far enough removed from them in time to look back upon them as a people amongst whom the golden age was apparent. They were accused of being stubborn, litigious, lazy or superstitious. It seems that they were stubborn, although they might be led where they could not be driven. The records indicate they were contentious, yet they were not unwilling to arbitrate their differences. They were perhaps not paragons of industry, but were probably industrious in the pursuit of modest comfort, and their wants were simple and easily satisfied on the fertile marshland without excessive labour. Some in closer contact with Europe considered that they were superstitious, but in general their priests seem to have been quite satisfied with their piety. They showed little passion for education, yet in an age when learning was restricted to the few they were probably no more illiterate than similar people in other places. Many of them had come from low-lying lands in the mother country, where they had been familiar with the technique of dyke-building, and that technique they put into practice on the marshlands at the mouths of tidal rivers in Acadia, particularly about the Basin of Minas and on the Isthmus of Chignecto.

In summer many of the men were employed in agriculture, in winter in wood cutting and hunting. Their gardens produced cabbages and 'all other sorts of pot herbs and vegetables.' The peas were 'so covered with pods that it could only be believed by seeing.' Wheat grew well, and apple and pear trees brought from France flourished. Fish were plentiful in stream and river. The Acadians also had large herds of cattle, yet 'they never made any merchantable butter, being used to set their milk in small noggins which were kept in such order as to turn it thick and sour in a short time, of which they ate voraciously.' The women displayed their fondness of colour, as well as an eagerness to obtain English scarlet cloth. In winter they busied themselves in carding, spinning and weaving wool, flax and hemp. With these materials and the furs of wild animals they made comfortable and in some cases colourful clothing.

A glimpse of that type of neutrality which became so evident among these people in the years between 1713 and 1755 may be found during the years between 1689 and 1697, which were a period of war between England

and France both in Europe and America. In that war the Acadians of the peninsula took no part, although Indian raids inspired in France and Quebec were directed against New England from Acadian soil, and a number of privateers procured supplies from Acadia and brought their booty back to it. Throughout those years, moreover, trade as usual continued unmolested between the Acadians and the New Englanders, while the French seat of government lay on the River St. John, first at Jemseg, then at Nashwaak and finally at the river mouth. The war indeed was a struggle over boundaries between New France and New England, and Acadia was little more than a pawn in the game. The French minister's view of Acadian neutrality was disclosed in his instructions to Villebon in 1696 that he was to inform the Acadians of Port Royal that the king had not given up the idea of protecting and sustaining them, that he should have them keep on good terms with the English only so far as would conduce to their preservation, and that they should not trade with them any more than was absolutely necessary.

The attitude of the Acadians with respect to war and government during the ensuing years of French control may be at least partly inferred from the comments of Governor de Brouillan. In October 1701 he reported that the inhabitants of Minas were so little accustomed to government that it seemed to him that they lived as republicans, recognizing neither royal authority nor justice. And two years later he declared that they plotted and, having assembled in arms, made resolutions tending towards a real sedition, and said publicly that they would submit to the English, if they presented themselves.

With the fall of Port Royal in 1710, the French seat of government, which had been there since 1701, fell to the English. By the terms of the capitulation it was agreed that the garrison should march out with the honours of war and be transported to France in English ships, and that the inhabitants within three miles of the fort should 'remain upon their estates with their corn, cattle, and furniture, during two years, in case they are not desirous to go before, they taking the oath of allegiance and fidelity to Her Sacred Majesty of Great Britain.'

The years between the surrender of Port Royal in 1710 and the signing of the Treaty of Utrecht in 1713 were a time of much difficulty and a period of considerable anxiety for the conquerors. In accordance with the terms of the capitulation, Governor Vetch administered the oath of allegiance to the inhabitants within the *banlieue,* an area within three miles of the fort, established a court to try disputes and endeavoured, as far as he was able, to set up military rule at Annapolis Royal. He had many problems to face: the Indians were hostile and, as might be expected in the state of war that still prevailed, emissaries of the French tried to keep the Acadians unfriendly to their English masters; the soldiers needed winter clothing, and their pay was in arrears; the fort needed repairs, and the military chest was empty. Receiving no assistance from Boston or London, the only resource left to Vetch seemed to be to levy on the inhabitants. This he did and, though the Acadians pleaded poverty, he succeeded, with the aid of armed men to enforce the order, in collecting at least a portion of the tribute not only from the inhabitants of the *banlieue* over whom he had authority, but also from the inhabitants of Minas and Chignecto, who were not included in the capitulation.

The first winter passed, not without some discomfort and privation, as well as anxiety, but without any serious mishap. The uncertainty of the situation of the inhabitants beyond the *banlieue* was a cause of uneasiness to them. They applied to the Governor for terms of protection, and offered, as Vetch reported, to take the oath of allegiance. His reply to them was that he could give them no terms until her Majesty's more particular orders were received; but that if they remained in peace he would not disturb them during the winter. In June, however, came a disaster. For a time the Acadians had complied with an order to cut timber for the repair of the fort and deliver it to Annapolis Royal. Then they quit work, fearing, as they said, the Indian allies of the French who threatened to kill them if they aided the enemy. Vetch thereupon ordered an officer to take seventy-five men and go up the river and inform the people that if they would bring down the timber they would receive protection, but if they were unwilling to do so, or delayed in so doing, to intimidate them. The troops set out, but they were ambushed by a war-party of French and Indians, and every one of the seventy-five was either killed or captured. Mascarene subsequently reported as follows: "The French after this changed their countenance and of humble and in appearance obedient turn'd haughty and imperious, and threaten'd no less than to take us by assault and put every one of us to the edge of the sword." Four days after the ambush, Vetch wrote as follows to Lord Dartmouth: ". . . As to the Civill state of affairs the Inhabitants in Generall as well French as Indians continue still in a great ferment and Uneasiness those within the Banlieue (who are but few) that have taken the oath of Alledgance to her Majesty are threatened and made uneasy by all the Others who call them Traytors and make them Believe the french will soon recover the place and then they will all be ruined." Thus the situation was critical, for the garrison was reduced by death and desertion. "The best that we thought on," stated Mascarene, "was to keep possession of what we had to wit Ye Fort and the lower town . . ." Precautions were accordingly taken, a trench was dug, and "no officer and but half of the soldiers and that in their Cloaths and with their arms by them were allowed to sleep at night butt the garrison could not have subsisted long under these fatigues and hardships—if news of Your Exys (Nicholson's) arrival at Boston and the vast fleet that followed had not rais'd the spirits now almost entirely sunk."

Elsewhere in 1711 the Canada expedition, which came to naught, was being prepared, but no aid arrived at Annapolis Royal until the following year when a band of Mohawks from New York came to aid the garrison. The Acadians, however, were in revolt; and as long as they cherished the belief that their countrymen would retrieve Acadia, all attempts to secure their allegiance to Queen Anne proved unavailing. Finally, in April 1713, the question of the ownership of the country was set at rest by the Treaty of Utrecht. By the terms of this treaty France was to retain Ile Royal (Cape Breton Island) and Ile St. Jean (Prince Edward Island), and to cede all Nova Scotia or Acadia "with its ancient limits" to the British.

The question of the oath of allegiance, the matter of the boundaries, and the views of the French and British governments towards one another, formed a background for developments in Nova Scotia between 1713 and 1755. By the terms of the Treaty of Utrecht the Acadians were to have liberty "to remove themselves within a year to any other place, as they shall think fit, together with all their moveable effects," and those who remained were "to be subject to the Kingdom of Great Britain" and "to enjoy the free exercise of their religion, according to the usage of the church of Rome, as far as the laws of Great Britain do allow the same." These terms were confirmed by a warrant of Queen Anne, dated 23 June 1713, and forwarded to Francis Nicholson by Lord Dartmouth. The Queen declared that as the King of France "hath at our desire released from Imprisonment on board his galleys, such of his subjects as were detained there on account of their professing the Protestant religion, we being willing to shew some mark of our favour towards his subjects how kindly we take his Complyance therein, have therefore thought fit hereby to signify our will & pleasure to you that you permit & allow such of them as have Lands or Tenem[ts] in the Places under your Government in Acadia & Newfoundland that have been or are to be yielded to us, by virtue of the late treaty of peace & are willing to continue our Subjects to retain & enjoy the sd Lands & Tenem[ts] without any Lett or Molestation as fully & freely as other our subjects do or may possess their Lands & Estates, or to sell the same if they shall rather chuse to remove elsewhere . . ."

After the Treaty of Utrecht the French government removed its garrison from Placentia in Newfoundland to Louisbourg in Ile Royale, where a mighty fortress was soon to be built, and endeavoured to induce the Acadians to go to that island, and to retain its influence over the Acadians and the Indians in Nova Scotia. Governor Vaudreuil of Canada sent Saint Castin to what is now New Brunswick with instructions to keep the Indians there in the French interest, and to persuade them that the lands were their own and not English territory, notwithstanding the cession of Acadia by the French king. As early as 23 September 1713, moreover, Felix Pain, the French missionary at Minas, informed Costebelle, governor of Ile Royal, that the Acadians were averse to leaving their lands in Nova Scotia, whence they drew their substence, without assistance, to go to Ile Royale, where they would have to clear new lands; but they would never take the oath of allegiance to the Queen of England to the prejudice of their king, their country and their religion; and they would leave their lands before violating in the slightest their fidelity to their king and their law.

On 30 November Costebelle, writing from Placentia to the Minister in France, indicated his distrust of the Acadians, and referred to them as selfish, idle people, and as having adopted the habits of the Indians. He advised against buying their aid, and stated that it would be better to purchase slaves. Meantime, on 5 November 1713, Colonel Caulfeild at Annapolis Royal reported that he had summoned all the inhabitants of that place, and signified to them Her Majesty's goodness to them, and that the principal inhabitants seemed extremely well satisfied and willing to continue in their plantations, "which in my humble opinion will be of Great Service to this Garrison & as for the others the sooner we are rid of them the better . . ."

In 1714 officers from Louisbourg visited the Acadian settlements in Nova Scotia and, with the permission of the British authorities, laid before the Acadians French proposals for their removal to Ile Royale. The Acadians were almost unanimous in signing declarations of their willingness to go. The French emissaries had requested that a year be allowed for the exodus, so that boats might be built and aid obtained from France to transport the goods and cattle. But the "year" of the Treaty of Utrecht had already elapsed, and Nicholson and his council of officers at Annapolis Royal, while willing to permit the fullest freedom and give every assistance to the French officers in meeting the Acadians, replied that their answer to that request must await instructions from England. During the winter the Lords of Trade in England considered the subject and, on the grounds that the loss of the Acadians and their cattle would mean ruin for the colony and an acquisition of strength to Louisbourg, whereas if they were retained they might provide a shield against the Indians, they decided that the Acadians should remain.

Matters drifted. After their first effort to induce the Acadians to go to Ile Royale, the French relapsed into inaction and saw the advantage of keeping the Acadians under French influence in British territory. In Europe, moreover, the weak and ill-established governments of Philip of Orleans, Regent of France, and of George I, King of England, needed peace for their security; and while, in ensuing years, these countries were allies in a struggle against Spain, the question about the Acadians and the oath of allegiance seemed of less moment.

On the accession of George I in 1715 the Acadians were requested to swear allegiance to the new monarch but they refused to do so; and when John Doucett arrived as lieutenant-governor in 1717 he was informed by the Acadians that "the French inhabitants had never own'd His Majesty as Possessor of this His Continent of Nova Scotia and L'Acadie." They declared their unwillingness to take such an oath until some means was afforded of protecting them from the Indians, and in case other means could not be found they were, they stated, ready to take up arms neither against His Britannic Majesty, nor France, nor any of their subjects or allies.

Meanwhile, the matter of the unconditional oath and the effect of French influence on the Acadians were subjects of concern for the British authorities. The Acadians were unwilling to take the oath without an exemption from bearing arms; and French influence seemed likely to continue in Nova Scotia as long as the priests among the Acadians were French rather than British subjects, paid by the French government and under the direction of the bishop of Quebec, and as long as the French were able to use to their advantage their alliance with the Indian tribes. When Governor Philipps arrived at Annapolis Royal in 1720, the Acadians of that district reported that they were not at liberty to swear allegiance because in Nicholson's time they had set their hands unanimously to an obligation of continuing subjects of France and of retiring to Cape Breton and, furthermore, they were sure of having their throats cut by the Indians "whenever they became Englishmen." They expressed their very great surprise "at the arrival of a Chief Governor which they never expected often saying that Person was not born . . ." "It is a hard and uneasy Task (in my circumstances)," Philipps wrote, "to manage a People, who will neither believe nor hearken to reason (unless it comes out of the mouths of their Priests) and at the same time to keep up the Honour and Dignity of Government." If the Acadians are permitted, Phillips added, "to remaine upon the Footing they propose it is very probable they will be Obedient to Government as long as the Two Crownes continue in Allyance but in case of a rupture will be so many Enemys in our Bosom and I cannot see any hopes or likelyhood of making them English unless it were possible to procure these Priests to be recalled who are Tooth and Naile against the Regent not sticking to say openly that it is his day now, but will be theirs anon, and having others sent in their stead, which (if anything) may contribute in a little time to make some changes in their sentiments and give them opportunity of opening their eyes, which hitherto are shutt even to their own Interest . . ." He also suggested a new form of land tenure for the Acadians, "instead of holding them as at present from the Lords of the Manor who are now at Cape Breton where at this day they pay their Rent." Hitherto, he said, this had been no more than "a Mock Government. It's authority having never yet extended beyond cannon reach of this Fort." As matters then stood, he thought it would be more to the honour of the Crown, and to its profit also, to give the country back to the French, than to be contented with the name only of government, and the charge that attends it, whilst they have the rule and make it subservient to the support of their settlement at Cape Breton.

An uneasy *modus vivendi* continued but the Acadians, who increased in numbers and profited from the demands of the garrison for their produce, as well as from smuggling with Cape Breton and trade with New England, were obdurate in their refusal to take the unconditional oath of allegiance. In 1720 Philipps called upon them to take the oath or leave the country within four months. They declined to take the oath, and were forbidden to cut a road by which they might leave. In 1726 Armstrong took up the matter again. He had little difficulty in the district of Annapolis, when he granted a clause exempting them from the obligation of taking up arms; but at Minas and Chignecto the inhabitants would take no oath but to their own good king of France. After the accession of George II in 1727 Ensign Wroth, who was commissioned to proclaim the king and obtain the submission of the people, promised them, on his own authority, freedom in the exercise of their religion, exemption from bearing arms and liberty to withdraw from the colony at any time. But Armstrong refused to ratify these concessions, and the Council declared them null and void, although they were of opinion that the inhabitants "having signed and proclaimed His Majesty and thereby acknowledged his title and authority to and over this Province, shall have the liberties and privileges of English subjects." That was all the Acadians desired. Wroth's commission however did not extend to the Annapolis district; and when its deputies were summoned to appear, they called a meeting on their own account, and passed a resolution offering to take the oath on the conditions granted by Wroth. This displeased the Council which ordered the arrest of the deputies, and forbade the rest from fishing on the British coasts. The action taken at Annapolis Royal and at the other settlements was therefore certainly not consistent.

In the absence of Governor Philipps from the coloney, his lieutenant, Armstrong, had some differences with the French priests, especially Abbé Breslay, with the result that when the Governor returned in 1729, and Armstrong obtained a leave of absence, Philipps was welcomed by the Acadians. He immediately confirmed Abbé Breslay in the parish, and the Acadians in the Annapolis district signified their pleasure at the changed circumstances by subscribing to the following oath: "I promise and swear on the faith of a Christian that I will be truly faithful and will submit myself to His Majesty King George the Second, whom I acknowledge as the lord and sovereign of Nova Scotia or Acadia." In the following spring Philipps obtained the submission of the inhabitants of the other districts, apparently after giving them an assurance that they would not have to take up arms against the French or the Indians. Now Philipps thought that he could congratulate the Lords of Trade on "the entire submission of all those so long obstinate People," and His Majesty "on the acquisition of so many subjects." But the triumph for Philipps' administration was more apparent than real for, as he himself stated, "to be secure in all Events requires further precautions for 'tis certain that all the Safety of this Province depends absolutely upon the continuance of that union (of the Crowns of Great Britain and France); when that ceases the Country becomes an easy prey to our Neighbours being in its present State not capable of much resistance and Canso (which is the envy and Rivall of Cape Breton in the fishery) will be sure of being the first attack'd which will take them no more than six or Seven hours to march and possess it." "But I am only the Watchman," he added, "to call and Point out the danger, 'tis with Your Lordships to get it prevented." He thought that now was the time to put the Acadians "upon some footing." It was, he thought, "a misfortune that we are not one Jott nearer to a Regular Form of Government by this Acquisition, their Religion disqualifying them from making a Part of the Legislature." Whether they should not pay towards the support of government, and in what degree, and whether they should not be obliged to take out new tenures for their lands from the Crown, "to which they are now become Subjects," were matters on which he awaited particular orders and instructions.

When the War of the Austrian Succession spread to America, after the French and English declarations of war in March and April, 1744, Philipps was proved right in his pointing out the danger to Canso. News of the war reached Louisbourg before it reached Boston, and Du Vivier from Louisbourg was, accordingly, able to surprise Canso and to take it without resistance. Later in the year a band of Indians, apparently accompanied by Abbé Maillard, marched against Annapolis Royal. Towards these raids the Acadians assumed an attitude of neutrality. They refused to join the Indians in their attack on Annapolis Royal; and when the Indians withdrew, on the arrival of aid from Boston, they returned to their work at the fort. When DuVivier and a French force also approached Annapolis Royal in that year, the Acadians aided them with provisions, but declared that DuVivier threatened them with punishment at the hands of the Indians if they did not do so. And when the French desired to winter at Chignecto, the Acadians objected and dissuaded them from so doing. In the month of May in the next year a force of Canadians and Indians invested Annapolis, and again the Acadians declined to take up arms, although they assisted the invaders with supplies.

Stung to action by such raids, New Englanders with the aid of a British naval squadron retaliated by capturing Louisbourg in 1745, and the French population there, both civil and military, was transported to France. In the following year, the French government sent the formidable D'Anville expedition across the Atlantic, with instructions to re-capture Louisbourg, to take Annapolis Royal, burn Boston, annoy and distress the English on the American coast, and finally to pay a visit to the English sugar islands in the West Indies. Storm, misfortune and disease took their toll of this expedition, although several ships reached Chebucto in Nova Scotia, where Le Loutre acted as intermediary between the fleet and Ramesay's Canadian troops, and it failed to achieve its objectives. Ramesay then retired to Chignecto, where he was joined by a band of Indians under Abbé Le Loutre, and tried to induce the Acadians to take up arms on the side of the French. New Englanders, under Col. Arthur Noble, were sent to the aid of Nova Scotia. In December these New Englanders, with a small number of soldiers from the garrison at Annapolis, set out to drive the Canadians from the colony. Having reached Grand Pré in the district of Minas, they decided to postpone their operations until the spring, and to spend the winter with the Acadians of Grand Pré. Notwithstanding the deep snow, the French force, having heard of Noble's position at Grand Pré, decided to surprise him by a forced march and a night attack. One midnight early in February the English were attacked, sixty of them were killed, seventy more wounded, and the rest surrendered. The French force then returned to Chignecto, and Ramesay issued a proclamation to the inhabitants of Grand Pré setting forth that "by virtue of conquest they now owed allegiance to the King of France," and warning them "to hold no communication with the inhabitants of Port Royal." But this proclamation had little effect, for with few exceptions the Acadians maintained their former attitude, and refused to take up arms on behalf of France even in the presence of French troops. Knowing the fate of the French who had been at Louisbourg, and hearing rumours that Canada was not only to be captured, but that they were to share a similar fate, the Acadians displayed some uneasiness. To allay their anxiety the Duke of Newcastle instructed Governor Shirley of Massachusetts to assure the Acadians "that there is not the least foundation for any apprehension of that nature: but that on the contrary it is His Majesty's resolution to protect and maintain all such of them as shall continue in their duty and allegiance to His Majesty in the quiet and peaceable possession of their habitations and settlements and that they shall continue to enjoy the free exercise of their religion." Although Shirley omitted the clause relating to religion from his proclamation, and explained that he did so for the sake of convenience, this proclamation, in the opinion of Mascarene, had a good effect.

Events of these years disclosed not only that Nova Scotia remained insecure, while the only settlers of British origin in the colony were the small British garrison at Annapolis Royal and, at times, a few soldiers as well as the fishermen at the summer fishing station at Canso, as long as the French maintained a base on Cape Breton Island, and could from Quebec exercise their influence and send their forces into the peninsula by way of the Isthmus of Chignecto. It had remained British only through the circumstances that the Acadians in the main were neutral, and because in crucial times New England reinforcements had been decisive. Indeed, New England influence was very important, for New England fishermen and traders had long been active in the colony or along its coasts, its citizens generally were sensitive to the coastal menace of a French Louisbourg, and its Governor, as well as others, including Mascarene, the administrator in Nova Scotia from 1740 to 1749, advocated making Nova Scotia a real barrier or shield for New England.

At last, in 1749, the British government, although it had restored Louisbourg to France by the Treaty of Aix-la-Chapelle in the previous year, made its first real attempt to colonize Nova Scotia, and established a settlement on the ocean-face of the colony at Halifax, which was intended not only as a counterpoise to Louisbourg, but also as a centre for trade and a base for the fishery. In that year about 2,700 settlers were brought out from England. Within a short time a considerable number of New Englanders took up residence there, and before very long New Englanders formed the largest element in the population. And between 1750 and 1753 two or three thousand "foreign Protestants" were brought from continental Europe to be given farms in Nova Scotia. But the menace from French and Indians forced the British authorities to keep these Europeans, at considerable expense, and no doubt to the immigrants' dissatisfaction, quartered for several years in the town of Halifax. Colonel Cornwallis, the new Governor of Nova Scotia, issued a proclamation containing "the declaration of His Majesty regarding the French inhabitants of Nova Scotia," and calling on the Acadians to take the oath of allegiance within three months. Again they refused to take the unqualified oath and, as had happened before, the Governor receded from his stand, on the ground that the Acadians, who had stated they would leave the colony before taking the oath, would not emigrate at that season, and that in the meantime he could use their services to advantage. Early in the next year moreover the French came again to the Isthmus of Chignecto, where they established themselves, and tried to restrict the British to only a part of the peninsula. If the Acadians should then leave the colony, they would add to the numbers as well as to the strength of an enemy near at hand and able to threaten the very existence of the British settlements. Thus it was that the question of the oath was still further postponed; and Cornwallis told the Acadians in 1750, when most of them declared for emigration, against their own inclination, but at the behest and under the threats of the French, that he would grant them permission to go as soon as there should be tranquillity, but in the present circumstances passports could be given to none. By that time the number of Acadians in Nova Scotia had increased from the less than 2,100 of the year 1710 to about 10,000.

With the founding of Halifax, French authorities at Louisbourg ordered Abbé Le Loutre, missionary to the Indians, to leave his headquarters at Shubenacadie, and withdraw his band to Beauséjour on the Isthmus. And when Col. Lawrence was sent to the Isthmus early in 1750, Le Loutre's Micmacs opposed his disembarkation, and the French troops under La Corne were so superior that Lawrence returned to Halifax with his troops and his settlers. Meantime Le Loutre, who had been unable to prevent the English from reaching the Acadian village of Beaubassin, and wished to preserve the Acadians from the contaminating presence of the English, went forward with his Indians and set fire to the village, thereby forcing its Acadian inhabitants to remove to the French camp at Beauséjour, a short distance away. Thus began the dispersion of the Acadians, who through great pressure from the French migrated in such numbers that by 1752 two thousand of them were to be found in Ile St. Jean, and about seven hundred in Ile Royale. Meantime in September 1750 Lawrence again reached Chignecto, where he established Fort Lawrence just across the river from Fort Beauséjour, notwithstanding the opposition of the Indians and a few Acadians. Shortly afterwards Captain Howe, one of the British officers, was murdered, under a flag of truce, probably by the Indians, and even such French citizens as Courville, the notary of Acadia, and Chevalier Johnstone, have charged Le Loutre with complicity in the deed.

When two thousand New England troops captured Fort Beauséjour in 1755, the year of Braddock's defeat, Governor Lawrence and his Council at Halifax decided that now was the time, while these troops were in Nova Scotia, and British ships were in the harbour, to settle the question of the Acadians and the oath of allegiance. Acadian deputies again refused to take the oath. Steps were taken to deport them from the colony, ships were hired, and the New England troops were used to carry out the decision. About that time there were approximately eight thousand Acadians in the peninsula and at the Isthmus. Six thousand of them were seized, and scattered throughout the British colonies from New England to St. Christopher, so that they might not be a menace to any one British colony, or be a source of strength to the French. About two thousand escaped the expulsion from Nova Scotia in 1755; and some who had gone earlier to Ile St. Jean were caught in the expulsion from that island in 1758, after it had been taken by the British, when others avoided it by fleeing to Quebec, Northern New Brunswick, to St. Pierre or to Miquelon. Governor Lawrence himself explained the situation in Nova Scotia as follows, in a letter dated 11 August of that year: "The success that has attended His Majesty's Armes in Driving the French from the Encroachments they had made in the Province, Furnished me with a Favourable opportunity of Reducing the French Inhabitants of this Colony, to a Proper Obedience to His Majesty and Governmente, or forcing them to quit the Country . . ."

The decision was perhaps a harsh one, and the enforcement of it was undoubtedly disagreeable even to some of those charged with carrying it out. Colonel Winslow, who was in command of the operation at

Grand Pré, in his proclamation to the Acadians there, used these words: "The Part of Duty I am now upon is what tho^{h} Necessary is Very Disagreeable to my Natural make & Temper as I know it Must be Grevious to you who are of the Same Specia."

Not many years after 1755 probably 2,000 of the exiled Acadians returned to Nova Scotia where, along with a like number who had escaped expulsion, they received grants of land, took the oath of allegiance, and assumed their full place in the life of the province. Others went to Quebec, Prince Edward Island, New Brunswick or other parts of the continent.

Looking back one sees that the Acadians of Nova Scotia maintained in the face of French and British policies a virtual neutrality, for but few joined the French in their aggressive designs, or aided them at the defense of Beauséjour in 1755. And, again looking back, it might appear that the expulsion was unnecessary, for if the old situation had persisted for only another five to eight years until the French menace on the continent had been eradicated, the problem would have no longer existed. Still further, in retrospect, one sees that the Acadians who remained, and those who returned, took the unqualified oath, accepted all the duties and received all the rights of citizens. If they could have taken such an oath prior to the events of 1755, those harsh deeds would not have been done. The fate of the Acadians hinged on international rivalry, and they were little more than pawns in the game.

C. Bruce Fergusson, M. A. (Oxon.)

Evangeline

A Tale of Acadie

THIS is the forest primeval. The murmuring pines and the hemlocks,
Bearded with moss, and in garments green, indistinct in the twilight,
Stand like Druids of eld, with voices sad and prophetic,
Stand like harpers hoar, with beards that rest on their bosoms.
Loud from its rocky caverns, the deep-voiced neighbouring ocean
Speaks, and in accents disconsolate answers the wail of the forest.

This is the forest primeval; but where are the hearts that beneath it
Leaped like the roe, when he hears in the woodland the voice of the huntsman?
Where is the thatch-roofed village, the home of Acadian farmers,—
Men whose lives glided on like rivers that water the woodlands,

Darkened by shadows of earth, but reflecting an image of heaven?
Waste are those pleasant farms, and the farmers for ever departed!
Scattered like dust and leaves, when the mighty blasts of October
Seize them, and whirl them aloft, and sprinkle them far o'er the ocean.
Naught but tradition remains of the beautiful village of Grand-Pré.
Ye who believe in affection that hopes, and endures, and is patient,
Ye who believe in the beauty and strength of woman's devotion,
List to the mournful tradition, still sung by the pines of the forest;
List to a Tale of Love in Acadie, home of the happy.

PART THE FIRST

I

IN the Acadian land, on the shores of the Basin of Minas,
Distant, secluded, still, the little village of Grand-Pré
Lay in the fruitful valley. Vast meadows stretched to the eastward,
Giving the village its name, and pasture to flocks without number.
Dikes, that the hands of the farmers had raised with labour incessant,
Shut out the turbulent tides; but at stated seasons the flood-gates
Opened, and welcomed the sea to wander at will o'er the meadows.
West and south there were fields of flax, and orchards and cornfields

Spreading afar and unfenced o'er the plain; and away to the northward
Blomidon rose, and the forests old, and aloft on the mountains
Sea-fogs pitched their tents, and mists from the mighty Atlantic
Looked on the happy valley, but ne'er from their station descended.
There, in the midst of its farms, reposed the Acadian village.
Strongly built were the houses, with frames of oak and of hemlock,
Such as the peasants of Normandy built in the reign of the Henries.
Thatched were the roofs, with dormer-windows; and gables projecting
Over the basement below protected and shaded the door-way.
There in the tranquil evenings of summer, when brightly the sunset
Lighted the village street, and gilded the vanes on the chimneys,
Matrons and maidens sat in snow-white caps and in kirtles
Scarlet and blue and green, with distaffs spinning the golden
Flax for the gossiping looms, whose noisy shuttles within doors
Mingled their sound with the whir of the wheels and the songs of the maidens.
Solemnly down the street came the parish priest, and the children
Paused in their play to kiss the hand he extended to bless them.
Reverend walked he among them; and up rose matrons and maidens,
Hailing his slow approach with words of affectionate welcome.

Then came the labourers home from the field, and serenely the sun sank
Down to his rest, and twilight prevailed. Anon from the belfry
Softly the Angelus sounded, and over the roofs of the village
Columns of pale blue smoke, like clouds of incense ascending,
Rose from a hundred hearths, the homes of peace and contentment.
Thus dwelt together in love these simple Acadian farmers,—
Dwelt in the love of God and of man. Alike were they free from
Fear, that reigns with the tyrant, and envy, the vice of republics.
Neither locks had they to their doors, nor bars to their windows;
But their dwellings were open as day and the hearts of the owners;
Their the richest was poor, and the poorest lived in abundance.

Somewhat apart from the village, and nearer the Basin of Minas,
Benedict Bellefontaine, the wealthiest farmer of Grand-Pré,
Dwelt on his goodly acres; and with him, directing his household,
Gentle Evangeline lived, his child, and the pride of the village.
Stalworth and stately in form was the man of seventy winters;
Hearty and hale was he, an oak that is covered with snowflakes;
White as the snow were his locks, and his cheeks as brown as the oak-leaves.

Fair was she to behold, that maiden of seventeen summers.
Black were her eyes as the berry that grows on the thorn by the way-side,
Black, yet how softly they gleamed beneath the brown shade of her tresses!
Sweet was her breath as the breath of kine that feed in the meadows.
When in the harvest heat she bore to the reapers at noontide
Flagons of home-brewed ale, ah! fair in sooth was the maiden.
Fairer was she when, on Sunday morn, while the bell from its turret
Sprinkled with holy sounds the air, as the priest with his hyssop
Sprinkles the congregation, and scatters blessings upon them,
Down the long street she passed, with her chaplet of beads and her missal,
Wearing her Norman cap, and her kirtle of blue, and the ear-rings,
Brought in the olden time from France, and since, as an heirloom,
Handed down from mother to child, through long generations.
But a celestial brightness — a more ethereal beauty—
Shone on her face and encircled her form, when, after confession,
Homeward serenely she walked with God's benediction upon her.
When she had passed, it seemed like the ceasing of exquisite music.

Firmly builded with rafters of oak, the house of the farmer

Stood on the side of a hill commanding the sea; and a shady
Sycamore grew by the door, with a woodbine wreathing around it.
Rudely carved was the porch, with seats beneath; and a footpath
Led through an orchard wide, and disappeared in the meadow.
Under the sycamore-tree were hives overhung by a penthouse,
Such as the traveller sees in regions remote by the road-side,
Built o'er a box for the poor, or the blessed image of Mary.
Farther down, on the slope of the hill, was the well with its moss-grown
Bucket, fastened with iron, and near it a trough for the horses.
Shielding the house from storms, on the north, were the barns and the farm-yard.
There stood the broad-wheeled wains and the antique ploughs and the harrows;
There were the folds for the sheep; and there, in his feathered seraglio,
Strutted the lordly turkey, and crowed the cock, with the self-same
Voice that in ages of old had startled the penitent Peter.
Bursting with hay were the barns, themselves a village. In each one
Far o'er the gable projected a roof of thatch; and a staircase,
Under the sheltering eaves, led up to the odorous corn-loft.
There too the dove-cot stood, with its meek and innocent inmates
Murmuring ever of love; while above in the variant breezes

Numberless noisy weathercocks rattled and sang of mutation.

Thus, at peace with God and the world, the farmer of Grand-Pré
Lived on his sunny farm, and Evangeline governed his household.
Many a youth, as he knelt in church and opened his missal,
Fixed his eyes upon her as the saint of his deepest devotion;
Happy was he who might touch her hand or the hem of her garment!
Many a suitor came to her door, by the darkness befriended,
And, as he knocked and waited to hear the sound of her footsteps,
Knew not which beat the louder, his heart or the knocker of iron;
Or at the joyous feast of the Patron Saint of the village,
Bolder grew, and pressed her hand in the dance as he whispered
Hurried words of love, that seemed a part of the music.
But, among all who came, young Gabriel only was welcome;
Gabriel Lajuenesse, the son of Basil the blacksmith,
Who was a mighty man in the village, and honoured of all men;
For, since the birth of time, throughout all ages and nations,
Has the craft of the smith been held in repute by the people.
Basil was Benedict's friend. Their children from earliest childhood
Grew up together as brother and sister; and Father Felician,

Priest and pedagogue both in the village, had taught them their letters
Out of the self-same book, with the hymns of the church and the plain-song.
But when the hymn was sung, and the daily lesson completed,
Swiftly they hurried away to the forge of Basil the blacksmith.
There at the door they stood, with wondering eyes to behold him
Take in his leathern lap the hoof of the horse as a plaything.
Nailing the shoe in its place; while near him the tire of the cart-wheel
Lay like a fiery snake, coiled round in a cirle of cinders
Oft on autumnal eves, when without in the gathering darkness
Bursting with light seemed the smithy, through every cranny and crevice,
Warm by the forge within they watched the labouring bellows,
And as its panting ceased, and the sparks expired in the ashes,
Merrily laughed, and said they were nuns going into the chapel.
Oft on sledges in winter, as swift as the swoop of the eagle,
Down the hillside bounding, they glided away o'er the meadow.
Oft in the barns they climbed to the populous nests on the rafters,
Seeking with eager eyes that wondrous stone, which the swallow
Brings from the shore of the sea to restore the sight of its fledglings;
Lucky was he who found that stone in the nest of the swallow!

Thus passed a few swift years, and they no longer were children.
He was a valiant youth, and his face, like the face of the morning,
Gladdened the earth with its light, and ripened thought into action.
She was a woman now, with the heart and hopes of a woman.
"Sunshine of Saint Eulalie" was she called; for that was the sunshine
Which, as the farmers believed, would load their orchards with apples;
She, too, would bring to her husband's house delight and abundance,
Filling it with love and the ruddy faces of children.

II

Now had the season returned, when the nights grow colder and longer,
And the retreating sun the sign of the Scorpion enters.
Birds of passage sailed through the leaden air, from the ice-bound,
Desolate northern bays to the shores of tropical islands.
Harvests were gathered in; and wild with the winds of September
Wrestled the trees of the forest, as Jacob of old with the angel.
All the signs foretold a winter long and inclement.
Bees, with prophetic instinct of want, had hoarded their honey
Till the hives overflowed; and the Indian hunters asserted
Cold would the winter be, for thick was the fur of the foxes.
Such was the advent of autumn. Then followed that beautiful season,

Called by the pious Acadian peasants the Summer of All-Saints!
Filled was the air with a dreamy and magical light; and the landscape
Lay as if new-created in all the freshness of childhood.
Peace seemed to reign upon earth, and the restless heart of the ocean
Was for a moment consoled. All sounds were in harmony blended.
Voices of children at play, the crowing of cocks in the farm-yards,
Whir of wings in the drowsy air, and the cooing of pigeons,
All were subdued and low as the murmurs of love, and the great sun
Looked with the eye of love through the golden vapours around him;
While arrayed in its robes of russet and scarlet and yellow,
Bright with the sheen of the dew, each glittering tree of the forest
Flashed like the plane-tree the Persian adorned with mantles and jewels.

Now recommenced the reign of rest and affection and stillness.
Day with its burden and heat had departed, and twilight descending
Brought back the evening star to the sky, and the herds to the homestead.
Pawing the ground they came, and resting their necks on each other,
And with their nostrils distended inhaling the freshness of evening.
Foremost, bearing the bell, Evangeline's beautiful heifer,

Proud of her snow-white hide, and the ribbon that waved from her collar,
Quietly paced and slow, as if conscious of human affection.
Then came the shepherd back with his bleating flocks from the sea-side,
Where was their favorite pasture. Behind them followed the watch-dog,
Patient, full of importance, and gained in the pride of his instinct,
Walking from side to side with a lordly air, and superbly
Waving his bushy tail, and urging forward the stragglers;
Regent of flocks was he when the shepherd slept; their protector,
When from the forest at night through the starry silence, the wolves howled.
Late, with the rising moon, returned the wains from the marshes,
Laden with briny hay, that filled the air with its odour.
Cheerily neighed the steeds, with dew on their manes and their fetlocks,
While aloft on their shoulders the wooden and ponderous saddles,
Painted with brilliant dyes, and adorned with tassels of crimson,
Nodded in bright array, like hollyhocks heavy with blossoms.
Patiently stood the cows meanwhile, and yielded their udders
Unto the milkmaid's hand; whilst loud and in regular cadence
Into the sounding pails the foaming streamlets descended.
Lowing of cattle and peals of laughter were heard in the farm-yard,

Echoed back by the barns. Anon they sank into stillness;
Heavily closed, with a jarring sound, the valves of the barn-doors,
Rattled the wooden bars, and all for a season was silent.

Indoors, warm by the wide-mouthed fireplace, idly the farmer
Sat in his elbow-chair, and watched how the flames and the smoke-wreaths
Struggled together like foes in a burning city. Behind him,
Nodding and mocking along the wall, with gestures fantastic,
Darted his own huge shadow, and vanished away into darkness.
Faces, clumsily carved in oak, on the back of his arm-chair
Laughed in the flickering light; and the pewter plates on the dresser
Caught and reflected the flame, as shields of armies the sunshine.
Fragments of song the old man sang, and carols of Christmas,
Such as at home, in the olden time, his fathers before him
Sang in their Norman orchards and bright Burgundian vineyards.
Close at her father's side was the gentle Evangeline seated,
Spinning flax for the loom, that stood in the corner behind her.
Silent awhile were its treadles, at rest was its diligent shuttle,
While the monotonous drone of the wheel, like the drone of a bagpipe,

Followed the old man's song and united the fragments together.
As in a church, when the chant of the choir at intervals ceases,
Footfalls are heard in the aisles, or words of the priest at the altar,
So, in each pause of the song, with measured motion the clock clicked.

Thus, as they sat, there were footsteps heard, and, suddenly lifted,
Sounded the wooden latch, and the door swung back on its hinges.
Benedict knew by the hob-nailed shoes it was Basil the blacksmith,
And by her beating heart Evangeline knew who was with him.
"Welcome!" the farmer exclaimed, as their footsteps paused on the threshold,
"Welcome, Basil, my friend! Come, take thy place on the settle
Close by the chimney-side, which is always empty without thee;
Take from the shelf overhead thy pipe and the box of tobacco;
Never so much thyself art thou as when through the curling
Smoke of the pipe or the forge thy friendly and jovial face gleams
Round and red as the harvest moon through the midst of the marshes."
Then, with a smile of content, thus answered Basil the blacksmith,
Taking with easy air the accustomed seat by the fireside:—
"Benedict Bellefontaine, thou hast ever thy jest and thy ballad!

Ever in the cheerfullest mood art thou, when others are filled with
Gloomy forebodings of ill, and see only ruin before them.
Happy art thou, as if every day thou hadst picked up a horseshoe."
Pausing a moment, to take the pipe that Evangeline brought him,
And with a coal from the embers had lighted, he slowly continued:—
"Four days now are passed since the English ships at their anchors
Ride in the Gaspereau's mouth, with their cannon pointed against us.
What their design may be is unknown; but all are commanded
On the morrow to meet in the church, where his Majesty's mandate
Will be proclaimed as law in the land. Alas! in the meantime
Many surmises of evil alarm the hearts of the people."
Then made answer the farmer:— "Perhaps some friendlier purpose
Brings these ships to our shores. Perhaps the harvests in England
By untimely rains or untimlier heat have been blighted,
And from our bursting barns they would feed their cattle and children."
"Not so thinketh the folk in the village," said, warmly, the blacksmith,
Shaking his head, as in doubt; then, heaving a sigh, he continued:—
"Louisbourg is not forgotten, nor Beau Séjour, nor Port Royal.
Many already have fled to the forest, and lurk on its outskirts.
Waiting with anxious hearts the dubious fate of to-morrow.

Arms have been taken from us, and warlike weapons of all kinds;
Nothing is left but the blacksmith's sledge and the scythe of the mower."
Then with a pleasant smile made answer the jovial farmer:—
"Safer are we unarmed, in the midst of our flocks and our cornfields,
Safer within these peaceful dikes, beseiged by the ocean,
Than our fathers in forts, beseiged by the enemy's cannon.
Fear no evil, my friend, and to-night may no shadow of sorrow
Fall on this house and hearth; for this is the night of the contract.
Built are the house and barn. The merry lads of the village
Strongly have built them and well; and, breaking the glebe round about them,
Filled the barn with hay, and the house with food for a twelvemonth.
René Leblanc will be here anon, with his papers and inkhorn.
Shall we not then be glad, and rejoice in the joy of our children?"
As apart by the window she stood, with her hand in her lover's,
Blushing Evangeline heard the words that her father had spoken,
And, as they died on his lips, the worthy notary entered.

III

Bent like a laboring oar, that toils in the surf of the ocean,

Bent, but not broken, by age was the form of the notary public;
Shocks of yellow hair, like the silken floss of the maize, hung
Over his shoulders; his forehead was high; and glasses with horn bows
Sat astride on his nose, with a look of wisdom supernal.
Father of twenty children was he, and more than a hundred
Children's children rode on his knee, and heard his great watch tick.
Four long years in the times of the war had he languished a captive,
Suffering much in an old French fort as the friend of the English.
Now, though warier grown, without all guile or suspicion,
Ripe in wisdom was he, but patient, and simple, and childlike.
He was beloved by all, and most of all by the children;
For he told them tales of the Loup-garou in the forest,
And of the goblin that came in the night to water the horses,
And of the white Létiche, the ghost of a child who unchristened
Died, and was doomed to haunt unseen the chambers of children;
And how on Christmas eve the oxen talked in the stable,
And how the fever was cured by a spider shut up in a nutshell,
And of the marvellous powers of four-leaved clover and horseshoes,
With whatsoever else was writ in the lore of the village.
Then up rose from his seat by the fireside Basil the blacksmith,
Knocked from his pipe the ashes, and slowly extending his right hand,

"Father LeBlanc," he exclaimed, "thou hast heard the talk in the village,
And perchance, canst tell us some news of these ships and their errand."
Then with modest demeanour made answer the notary public,
"Gossip enough have I heard, in sooth, yet am never the wiser;
And what their errand may be I know not better than others.
Yet am I not of those who imagine some evil intention
Brings them here, for we are at peace; and why then molest us?"
"God's name!" shouted the hasty and somewhat irascible blacksmith;
"Must we in all things look for the how, and the why, and the wherefore?
Daily injustice is done, and might is the right of the strongest!"
But without heeding his warmth, continued the notary public—
"Man is unjust, but God is just; and finally justice
Triumphs; and well I remember a story, that often consoled me,
When as a captive I lay in the old French fort at Port Royal."
This was the old man's favorite tale, and he loved to repeat it
When his neighbours complained that any injustice was done them.
"Once in an ancient city, whose name I no longer remember,
Raised aloft on a column, a brazen statue of Justice
Stood in the public square, upholding the scales in its left hand,
And in its right a sword, as an emblem that justice presided

Over the laws of the land, and the hearts and homes of the people.
Even the birds had built their nests in the scales of the balance,
Having no fear of the sword that flashed in the sunshine above them.
But in the course of time the laws of the land were corrupted;
Might took the place of right, and the weak were oppressed, and the mighty
Ruled with an iron rod. Then it chanced in a nobleman's palace
That a necklace of pearls was lost, and ere long a suspicion
Fell on an orphan girl who lived as a maid in the household.
She, after form of trial, condemned to die on the scaffold,
Patiently met her doom at the foot of the statue of Justice.
As to her Father in Heaven her innocent spirit ascended,
Lo! o'er the city a tempest rose; and the bolts of the thunder
Smote the statue of bronze, and hurled in wrath from its left hand
Down on the pavement below the clattering scales of the balance,
And in the hollow thereof was found the nest of a magpie,
Into whose clay-built walls the necklace of pearls was inwoven."
Silenced, but not convinced, when the story was ended, the blacksmith
Stood like a man who fain would speak, but findeth no language;

All his thoughts were congealed into lines on his face, as the vapours
Freeze in fantastic shapes on the window-panes in the winter.

Then Evangeline lighted the brazen lamp on the table,
Filled, till it overflowed, the pewter tankard with home-brewed
Nut-brown ale, that was famed for its strength in the village of Grand-Pré;
While from his pocket the notary drew his papers and inkhorn,
Wrote with a steady hand the date and the age of the parties,
Naming the dower of the bride in flocks of sheep and in cattle.
Orderly all things proceeded, and duly and well were completed,
And the great seal of the law was set like a sun on the margin.
Then from his leathern pouch the farmer threw on the table
Three times the old man's fee in solid pieces of silver;
And the notary rising, and blessing the bride and the bridegroom,
Lifted aloft the tankard of ale and drank to their welfare.
Wiping the foam from his lip, he solemnly bowed and departed,
While in silence the others sat and mused by the fireside,
Till Evangeline brought the draughtboard out of its corner.
Soon was the game begun. In friendly contention the old men

Laughed at each lucky hit, or unsuccessful manoeuvre,
Laughed when a man was crowned, or a breach was made in the king-row.
Meanwhile, apart, in the twilight gloom of a window's embrasure,
Sat the lovers, and whispered together, beholding the moon rise
Over the pallid sea and the silvery mist of the meadows.
Silently one by one, in the infinite meadows of heaven,
Blossomed the lovely stars, the forget-me-nots of the angels.

Thus was the evening passed. Anon the bell from the belfry
Rang out the hour of nine, the village curfew, and straightway
Rose the guests and departed; and silence reigned in the household.
Many a farewell word and sweet goodnight on the doorstep
Lingered long in Evangeline's heart, and filled it with gladness.
Carefully then were covered the embers that glowed on the hearth-stone,
And on the oaken stairs resounded the tread of the farmer.
Soon with a soundless step the foot of Evangeline followed.
Up the staircase moved a luminous space in the darkness,
Lighted less by lamp than the shining face of the maiden.
Silent she passed the hall, and entered the door of her chamber.
Simple that chamber was, with its curtains of white, and its clothespress

Ample and high, on whose spacious shelves were carefully folded
Linen and woollen tuffs, by the hand of Evangeline woven.
This was the precious dower she would bring to her husband in marriage,
Better than flocks and herds, being proofs of her skill as a housewife.
Soon she extinguished her lamp, for the mellow and radiant moonlight
Streamed through the windows, and lighted the room, till the heart of the maiden
Swelled and obeyed its power, like the tremulous tides of the ocean.
Ah! she was fair, exceeding fair to behold, as she stood with
Naked snow-white feet on the gleaming floor of her chamber!
Little she dreamed that below, among the trees of the orchard,
Waited her lover and watched for the gleam of her lamp and her shadow.
Yet were her thoughts of him, and at times a feeling of sadness
Passed o'er her soul, as the sailing shade of clouds in the moonlight
Flitted across the floor and darkened the room for a moment.
And, as she gazed from the window, she saw serenely the moon pass.
Forth from the folds of a cloud, and one star follow her footsteps,
As out of Abraham's tent young Ishmael wandered with Hagar!

IV

Pleasantly rose next morn the sun on the village of Grand-Pré.
Pleasantly gleamed in the soft, sweet air the Basin of Minas,
Where the ships, with their wavering shadows, were riding at anchor.
Life had long been astir in the village, and clamorous labor
Knocked with its hundred hands at the golden gates of the morning.
Now from the country around, from the farms and neighboring hamlets,
Came in their holiday dresses the blithe Acadian peasants.
Many a glad good-morrow and jocund laugh from the young folk
Made the bright air brighter, as up from the numerous meadows,
Where no path could be seen but the track of wheels in the greenward,
Group after group appeared, and jointed, or passing on the highway.
Long ere noon, in the village all sounds of labour were silenced.
Thronged were the streets with people; and noisy groups at the house-doors
Sat in the cheerful sun, and rejoiced and gossiped together.
Every house was an inn, where all were welcomed and feasted;
For with this simple people, who lived like brothers together,
All things were held in common, and what one had was another's.
Yet under Benedict's roof hospitality seemed more abundant:

For Evangeline stood among the guests of her father;
Bright was her face with smiles, and words of welcome and gladness
Fell from her beautiful lips, and blessed the cup as she gave it.
Under the open sky, in the odorous air of the orchard,
Stript of its golden fruit, was spread the feast of betrothal.
There in the shade of the porch were the priest and the notary seated;
There good Benedict sat, and sturdy Basil the blacksmith.
Not far withdrawn from these, by the cider-press and the beehives,
Michael the fiddler was placed, with the gayest of hearts and of waistcoats.
Shadow and light from the leaves alternately played on his snow-white
Hair, as it waved in the wind; and the jolly face of the fiddler
Glowed like a living coal when the ashes are blown from the embers.
Gaily the old man sang to the vibrant sound of his fiddle,
"Tous les Bourgeois de Chartres," and *"Le Carillon de Dunkerque."*
And anon with his wooden shoes beat time to the music.
Merrily, merrily whirled the wheels of the dizzying dances
Under the orchard-trees and down the path to the meadows;
Old folk and young together, and children mingled among them.
Fairest of all the maids was Evangeline, Benedict's daughter!
Noblest of all the youths was Gabriel, son of the blacksmith!

So passed the morning away. And lo! with a summons sonorous
Sounded the bell from its tower, and over the meadows a drum beat.
Thronged ere long was the church with men. Without, in the churchyard,
Waited the women. They stood by the graves, and hung on the head-stones
Garlands of autumn-leaves and evergreens fresh from the forest.
Then came the guard from the ships, and marching proudly among them
Entered the sacred portal. With loud and dissonant clangour
Echoed the sound of their brazen drums from ceiling and casement,—
Echoed a moment only, and slowly the ponderous portal
Closed, and in silence the crowd awaited the will of the soldiers.
Then uprose their commander, and spake from the steps of the altar,
Holding aloft in his hands, with its seals, the royal commission.
"You are convened this day," he said, "by his Majesty's orders.
Clement and kind has he been; but how you have answered his kindness,
Let your own hearts reply! To my natural make and my temper
Painful the task is I do, which to you I know must be grievous.
Yet must I bow and obey, and deliver the will of our monarch;
Namely, that all your lands, and dwellings, and cattle of all kinds,
Forfeited be to the crown; and that you yourselves from this province

Be transported to other lands. God grant you may dwell there
Ever be faithful subjects, a happy and peaceable people!
Prisoners now I declare you; for such is his Majesty's pleasure!"
As, when the air is serene in the sultry solstice of summer,
Suddenly gathers a storm, and the deadly sling of the hailstones
Beats down the farmer's corn in the field and shatters his windows,
Hiding the sun, and strewing the ground with thatch from the house-roofs,
Bellowing fly the herds, and seek to break their enclosures;
So on the hearts of the people descended the words of the speaker.
Silent a moment they stood in speechless wonder, and then rose
Louder and ever louder a wail of sorrow and anger,
And, by one impulse moved, they madly rushed to the doorway.
Vain was the hope of escape; and cries and fierce imprecations
Rang through the house of prayer; and high o'er the heads of the others
Rose, with his arms uplifted, the figure of Basil the blacksmith,
As, on a stormy sea, a spar is tossed by the billows.
Flushed was his face and distorted with passion; and wildly he shouted,—
"Down with the tyrants of England! we never have sworn them allegiance!
Death to these foreign soldiers, who seize on our homes and our harvests!"
More he fain would have said, but the merciless hand of a soldier

Smote him upon the mouth, and dragged him down to the pavement.

In the midst of the strife and tumult of angry contention,
Lo! the door of the chancel opened, and Father Felician
Entered with serious mien, and ascended the steps of the altar.
Raising his reverend hand, with a gesture he awed into silence
All that clamorous throng; and thus he spake to his people;
Deep were his tones and solemn in accents measured and mournful
Spake he, as, after the tocsin's alarm, distinctly the clock strikes.
"What is this that ye do, my children? what madness has seized you?
Forty years of my life have I laboured among you, and taught you,
Not in word alone, but in deed, to love one another!
Is this the fruit of my toils, of my vigils and prayers and privations?
Have you so soon forgotten all lessons of love and forgiveness?
This is the house of the Prince of Peace, and would you profane it
Thus with violent deeds and hearts overflowing with hatred?
Lo! where the crucified Christ from His cross is gazing upon you!
See! in those sorrowful eyes what meekness and holy compassion!
Hark! how those lips still repeat the prayer, 'O Father, forgive them!'
Let us repeat that prayer in the hour when the wicked assail us.

Let us repeat it now, and say, O Father, forgive them!"
Few were his words of rebuke, but deep in the hearts of his people
Sank they, and sobs of contrition succeeded that passionate outbreak,
And they repeated his prayer, and said, "O Father, forgive them!"

Then came the evening service. The tapers gleamed from the altar.
Fervent and deep was the voice of the priest, and the people responded,
Not with their lips alone, but their hearts; and the Ave Maria
Sang they, and fell on their knees, and their souls, with devotion translated,
Rose on the ardour of prayer, like Elijah ascending to heaven.

Meanwhile had spread in the village the tidings of ill, and on all sides
Wandered, wailing, from house to house the women and children.
Long at her father's door Evangeline stood, with her right hand
Shielding her eyes from the level rays of the sun, that, descending,
Lighted the village street with mysterious splendour, and roofed each
Peasant's cottage with golden thatch, and emblazoned its windows.
Long within had been spread the snow-white cloth on the table;
There stood the wheaten loaf, and the honey fragrant with wild flowers;

There stood the tankard of ale, and the cheese, fresh brought from the dairy,
And, at the head of the board, the great arm-chair of the farmer.
Thus did Evangeline wait at her father's door, as the sunset
Threw the long shadows of trees o'er the broad ambrosial meadows.
Ah! on her spirit within a deeper shadow had fallen,
And from the fields of her soul a fragrance celestial ascended,—
Charity, meekness, love, and hope, and forgiveness, and patience!
Then, all forgetful of self, she wandered into the village,
Cheering with looks and words the mournful hearts of the women,
As o'er the darkening fields with lingering steps they departed,
Urged by their household cares, and the weary feet of their children.
Down sank the great red sun, and in golden, glimmering vapours
Veiled the light of his face, like the Prophet descending from Sinai.
Sweetly over the village the bell of the Angelus sounded.

Meanwhile, amid the gloom, by the church Evangeline lingered.
All was silent within; and in vain at the door and the windows
Stood she, and listened and looked, till, overcome by emotion,
"Gabriel!" cried she aloud with tremulous voice; but no answer
Came from the graves of the dead, nor the gloomier grave of the living.

Henry Wadsworth Longfellow

The memorial church at Grand Pré National Park, Nova Scotia. Photo by Sherman Hines.

The Acadian communities that grew up around the Bay of Fundy based their agriculture on reclaimed marshland. Dykes held back the highest tides from the upper reaches of the saltmarsh and permitted the cultivation of large areas of wheat. Illustration courtesy of the Public Archives of Canada.

When in the harvest heat she bore to the reapers
at noontide
Flagons of home-brewed ale, ah! fair in sooth
was the maiden

Illustration by Frank Dicksee. From *Evangeline: the Place, the Story, the Poem.* Cassell, Petter, Galpin & Co., New York, 1882. In the collection of the Nova Scotia Legislative Library.

Meanwhile, apart, in the twilight gloom of a
window's embrasure,
Sat the lovers, and whispered together,
beholding the moonrise.

Illustration by F.O.C. Darley. From *Evangeline*. Houghton Mifflin and Co., Boston, 1893. In the collection of the Nova Scotia Legislative Library.

Fairest of all the maids was Evangeline,
Benedict's daughter!
Noblest of all the youths was Gabriel,
son of the blacksmith!

Still from the motion picture *Evangeline: A Romance of Acadia*, circa 1920.

Vain was the hope of escape; and cries and
fierce imprecations
Rang through the house of prayer...

Illustration by Jesse Wilcox Smith. From *Evangeline*. Houghton Mifflin and Co., Boston, 1897. In the collection of the Nova Scotia Legislative Library.

Came from the neighbouring hamlets and farms the Acadian women,
Driving in ponderous wains their household goods to the seashore.

Illustration by Frank Dicksee. From *Evangeline: the Place, the Story, the Poem.* Cassell, Petter, Galpin & Co., New York, 1882. In the collection of the Nova Scotia Legislative Library.

Gabriel! be of good cheer! for if we love one
another,
Nothing in truth, can harm us, whatever mischances
may happen!

Illustration by C.W. Jefferies. Courtesy of the Public Archives of Canada.

And, as a signal sound, if others like them peradventure
Sailed on those gloomy and midnight streams, blew a blast on his bugle.

Illustration by F.O.C. Darley. From *Evangeline*. Houghton Mifflin and Co., Boston, 1866. In the collection of the Nova Scotia Legislative Library.

Sometimes they saw, or thought they saw, the smoke of his campfire.

Illustration by F.O.C. Darley. From *Evangeline*. Houghton Mifflin and Co., Boston, 1893. In the Collection of the Nova Scotia Legislative Library.

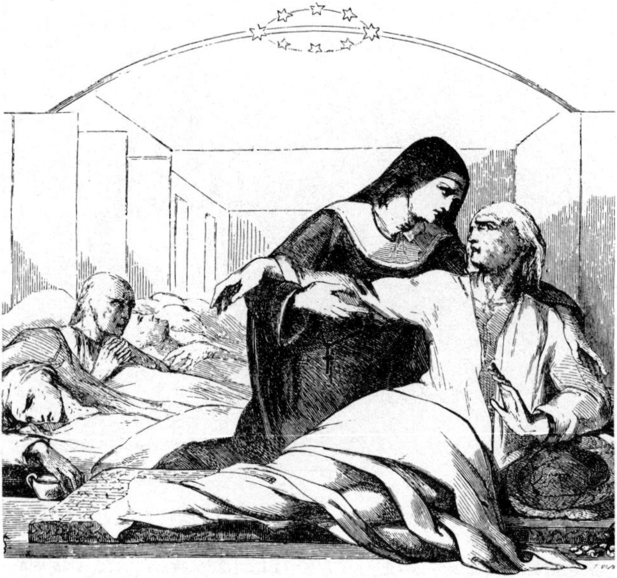

Vainly he strove to rise; and Evangeline,
kneeling beside him,
Kissed his dying lips, and laid his head
on her bosom.

Illustration by Jane E. Bentham. From *Evangeline*. David Bogue publisher, London, 1850. In the Collection of the Nova Scotia Legislative Library.

Slowly at length she returned to the tenantless house of her father.
Smouldered the fire on the hearth, on the board was the supper untasted,
Empty and drear was each room, and haunted with phantoms of terror.
Sadly echoed her step on the stair and the floor of her chamber.
In the dead of the night she heard the disconsolate rain fall
Loud on the withered leaves of the sycamore-tree by the window.
Keenly the lightning flashed; and the voice of the echoing thunder
Told her that God was in heaven, and governed the world he created!
Then she remembered the tale she had heard of the justice of Heaven;
Soothed was her troubled soul, and she peacefully slumbered till morning.

V

Four times the sun had risen and set; and now on the fifth day
Cheerily called the cock to the sleeping maids of the farm-house.
Soon o'er the yellow fields, in silent and mournful procession,
Came from the neighbouring hamlets and farms the Acadian women,
Driving in ponderous wains their household goods to the sea-shore,
Pausing and looking back to gaze once more on their dwellings,
Ere they were shut from sight by the winding road and the woodland.

Close at their sides their children ran, and urged on the oxen,
While in their little hands they clasped some fragments of playthings.

Thus, to the Gaspereau's mouth they hurried; and there on the sea-beach
Piled in confusion lay the household goods of the peasants.
All day long between the shore and the ships did the boats ply;
All day long the wains came labouring down from the village.
Late in the afternoon, when the sun was near to his setting,
Echoed far o'er the fields came the roll of drums from the church-yard.
Thither the women and children thronged. On a sudden the church doors
Opened, and forth came the guard, and marching in gloomy procession
Followed the long imprisoned, but patient, Acadian farmers.
Even as pilgrims, who journey afar from their homes and their country,
Sing as they go, and in singing forget they are weary and way-worn,
So with songs on their lips the Acadian peasants descended
Down from the church to the shore, amid their wives and their daughters.
Foremost the young men came; and, raising together their voices,
Sang they with tremulous lips a chant of the Catholic Missions:—
"Sacred heart of the Saviour! O inexhaustible fountain!
Fill our hearts this day with strength and submission and patience!"

Then the old men, as they marched, and the women that stood by the way-side,
Joined in the sacred psalm, and the birds in the sunshine above them
Mingled their notes therewith, like voices of spirits departed.

Half-way down to the shore Evangeline waited in silence,
Not overcome with grief, but strong in the hour of affliction,—
Calmly and sadly she waited, until the procession approached her,
And she beheld the face of Gabriel pale with emotion.
Tears then filled her eyes, and, eagerly running to meet him,
Clasped she his hands, and laid her head on his shoulder, and whispered,—
"Gabriel! be of good cheer! for if we love one another,
Nothing, in truth, can harm us, whatever mischances may happen!"
Smiling she spake these words; then suddenly paused, for her father
Saw she slowly advancing. Alas! how changed was his aspect!
Gone was the glow from his cheek, and the fire from his eye, and his footstep
Heavier seemed with the weight of the heavy heart in his bosom.
But, with a smile and a sigh, she clasped his neck and embraced him,
Speaking words of endearment where words of comfort availed not.
Thus to the Gaspereau's mouth moved on that mournful procession.

There disorder prevailed, and the tumult and stir of embarking.
Busily plied the freighted boats; and in the confusion
Wives were torn from their husbands, and mothers, too late, saw their children
Left on the land, extending their arms, with wildest entreaties.
So unto separate ships were Basil and Gabriel carried,
While in despair on the shore Evangeline stood with her father.
Half the task was not done when the sun went down, and the twilight
Deepened and darkened around; and in haste the refluent ocean
Fled away from the shore, and left the line of the sand-beach
Covered with waifs of the tide, with kelp and the slippery sea-weed.
Farther back in the midst of the household goods and the wagons,
Like to a gipsy camp, or a leaguer after a battle,
All escape cut off by the sea, and the sentinels near them,
Lay encamped for the night the houseless Acadian farmers.
Back to its nethermost caves retreated the bellowing ocean,
Dragging adown the beach the rattling pebbles, and leaving
Inland and far up the shore the stranded boats of the sailors.
Then, as the night descended, the herds returned from their pastures;
Sweet was the moist still air with the odour of milk from their udders;
Lowing they waited, and long, at the well-known bars of the farm-yard,—

Waited and looked in vain for the voice and the hand of the milkmaid.
Silence reigned in the street; from the church no Angelus sounded,
Rose no smoke from the roofs, and gleamed no lights from the windows.

But on the shores meanwhile the evening fires had been kindled,
Built of the drift-wood thrown on the sands from wrecks in the tempest.
Round them shapes of gloom and sorrowful faces were gathered,
Voices of women were heard, and of men, and the crying of children.
Onward from fire to fire, as from hearth to hearth in his parish,
Wandered the faithful priest, consoling and blessing and cheering,
Like unto shipwrecked Paul on Melita's desolate seashore.
Thus he approached the place where Evangeline sat with her father.
And in the flickering light beheld the face of the old man,
Haggard and hollow and wan, and without either thought or emotion.
E'en as the face of a clock from which the hands have been taken.
Vainly Evangeline strove with words and caresses to cheer him,
Vainly offered him food; yet he moved not, he looked not, he spake not,
But, with a vacant stare, ever gazed at the flickering fire-light.
"Benedicite!" murmured the priest, in tones of compassion.

More he fain would have said, but his heart was full, and his accents
Faltered and paused on his lips, as the feet of a child on a threshold,
Hushed by the scene he beholds, and the awful presence of sorrow.
Silently, therefore, he laid his hand on the head of the maiden,
Raising his tearful eyes to the silent stars that above them
Moved on their way, unperturbed by the wrongs and sorrows of mortals.
Then sat he down at her side, and they wept together in silence.

Suddenly rose from the south a light, as in autumn the blood-red
Moon climbs the crystal walls of heaven, and o'er the horizon
Titan-like stretches its hundred hands upon mountain and meadow,
Seizing the rocks and the rivers, and piling huge shadows together.
Broader and ever broader it gleamed on the roofs of the village,
Gleamed on the sky and the sea, and the ships that lay in the roadstead.
Columns of shining smoke uprose, and flashes of flame were
Thrust through their folds and withdrawn like the quivering hands of a martyr.
Then as the winds seized the gleeds and the burning thatch and uplifting,
Whirled them aloft through the air, at once from a hundred housetops
Started the sheeted smoke with ashes of flame intermingled.

These things beheld in dismay the crowd on the shore and on shipboard.
Speechless at first they stood, then cried aloud in their anguish,
"We shall behold no more our homes in the village of Grand-Pré!"
Loud on a sudden the cocks began to crow in the farm-yards,
Thinking the day had dawned; and anon the lowing of cattle
Came on the evening breeze, by the barking of dogs interrupted.
Then rose the sound of dread, such as startles the sleeping encampments
Far in the western prairies of forests that skirt the Nebraska,
When the wild horses affrighted sweep by with the speed of the whirlwind,
Or the loud bellowing herds of buffaloes rush to the river.
Such was the sound that arose on the night, as the herds and the horses
Broke through their folds and fences, and madly rushed o'er the meadows.

Overwhelmed with the sight, yet speechless, the priest and the maiden
Gazed on the scene of terror that reddened and widened before them;
And as they turned at length to speak to their silent companion,
Lo! from his seat he had fallen, and stretched abroad on the seashore
Motionless lay his form, from which the soul had departed.
Slowly the priest uplifted the lifeless head, and the maiden

Knelt at her father's side, and wailed aloud in her terror.
Then in a swoon she sank, and lay with her head on his bosom.
Through the long night she lay in deep, oblivious slumber;
And when she awoke from the trance, she beheld a multitude near her.
Faces of friends she beheld, that were mournfully gazing upon her;
Pallid, with tearful eyes, and looks of saddest compassion.
Still the blaze of the burning village illumined the landscape,
Reddened the sky overhead, and gleamed on the faces around her,
And like the day of doom it seemed to her wavering senses.
Then a familiar voice she heard, as it said to the people,—
"Let us bury him here by the sea. When a happier season
Brings us again to our home from the unknown land of our exile,
Then shall his sacred dust be piously laid in the churchyard."
Such were the words of the priest. And there in haste by the seaside,
Having the glare of the burning village for funeral torches,
But without bell or book, they buried the farmer of Grand-Pré.
And as the voice of the priest repeated the service of sorrow,
Lo! with a mournful sound, like the voice of a vast congregation,
Solemnly answered the sea, and mingled its roar with the dirges.

Twas the returning tide, that afar from the waste of the ocean,
With the first dawn of the day, came heaving and hurrying landward.
They recommenced once more the stir and noise of embarking;
And with the ebb of the tide the ships sailed out of the harbour,
Leaving behind them the dead on the shore, and the village in ruins.

PART THE SECOND

I

Many a weary year had passed since the burning of Grand-Pré,
When on the falling tide the freighted vessels departed,
Bearing a nation, with all its household goods, into exile,
Exile without an end, and without an example in story.
Far asunder, on separate coasts, the Acadians landed;
Scattered were they, like flakes of snow, when the wind from the north-east
Strikes aslant through the fogs that darken the Banks of Newfoundland.
Friendless, homeless, hopeless, they wandered from city to city,
From the cold lakes of the North to sultry Southern savannas,—
From the bleak shores of the sea to the lands where the Father of Waters
Seizes the hills in his hands, and drags them down to the ocean,
Deep in their sands to bury the scattered bones of the mammoth.

Friends they sought and homes; and many, despairing, heart-broken,
Asked of the earth but a grave, and no longer a friend nor a fireside.
Written their history stands on tablets of stone in the churchyards.
Long among them was seen a maiden who waited and wandered,
Lowly and meek in spirit, and patiently suffering all things.
Fair was she and young; but, alas! before her extended,
Dreary and vast and silent, the desert of life, with its pathway
Marked by the graves of those who had sorrowed and suffered before her,
Passions long extinguished, and hopes long dead and abandoned,
As the emigrant's way o'er the Western desert is marked by
Camp-fires long consumed, and bones that bleach in the sunshine.
Something there was in her life incomplete, imperfect, unfinished;
As if a morning of June, with all its music and sunshine,
Suddenly paused in the sky, and, fading, slowly descended
Into the east again, from whence it late had arisen.
Sometimes she lingered in towns, till, urged by the fever within her,
Urged by a restless longing, the hunger and thirst of the spirit,
She would commence again her endless search and endeavour;
Sometimes in churchyards strayed, and gazed on the crosses and tombstones,
Sat by some nameless grave, and thought that perhaps in its bosom

He was already at rest, and she longed to slumber beside him.
Sometimes a rumour, a hearsay, an inarticulate whisper,
Came with its airy hand to point and beckon her forward.
Sometimes she spake with those who had seen her beloved and known him,
But it was long ago, in some far-off place or forgotten.
"Gabriel Lajeunesse!" they said; "Oh yes! we have seen him.
He was with Basil the blacksmith, and both have gone to the prairies;
Coureurs-des-Bois are they, and famous hunters and trappers."
"Gabriel Lajeunesse!" said others; "Oh yes! we have seen him.
He is a Voyageur in the lowlands of Louisiana."
Then they would say,—"Dear child! why dream and wait for him longer?
Are there not other youths as fair as Gabriel? others
Who have hearts as tender and true, and spirits as loyal?
Here is Baptiste Leblanc, the notary's son, who had loved thee
Many a tedious year; come, give him thy hand and be happy!
Thou art too fair to be left to braid St. Catherine's tresses."
Then would Evangeline answer, serenely but sadly,—"I cannot!
Whither my heart has gone, there follows my hand, and not elsewhere.
For when the heart goes before, like a lamp, and illumines the pathway,
Many things are made clear, that else lie hidden in darkness."

Thereupon the priest, her friend and father-confessor,
Said, with a smile,—"O daughter! thy God thus speaketh within thee!
Talk not of wasted affection, affection never was wasted;
If it enrich not the heart of another, its waters, returning
Back to their springs, like the rain, shall fill them full of refreshment;
That which the fountain sends forth returns again to the fountain.
Patience; accomplish thy labor; accomplish thy work of affection!
Sorrow and silence are strong, and patient endurance is godlike.
Purified, strengthened, perfected, and rendered more worthy of heaven!"
Cheered by the good man's words, Evangeline laboured and waited.
Still in her heart she heard the funeral dirge of the ocean,
But with its sound there was mingled a voice that whispered, "Despair not!"
Thus did that poor soul wander in want and cheerless discomfort,
Bleeding, barefooted, over the shards and thorns of existence.
Let me essay, O Muse! to follow the wanderer's footsteps;—
Not through each devious path, each changeful year of existence,
But as a traveller follows a streamlet's course through the valley:
Far from its margin at times, and seeing the gleam of its water
Here and there, in some open space, and at intervals only;
Then drawing nearer its banks, through sylvan glooms that conceal it,

Though he behold it not, he can hear its continuous murmur;
Happy, at length, if he find the spot where it reaches an outlet.

II

It was the month of May. Far down the Beautiful River,
Past the Ohio shore and past the mouth of the Wabash,
Into the golden stream of the broad and swift Mississippi,
Floated a cumbrous boat, that was rowed by Acadian boatmen.
It was a band of exiles: a raft, as it were, from the shipwrecked
Nation, scattered along the coast, now floating together,
Bound by the bonds of a common belief and a common misfortune;
Men and women and children, who, guided by hope or by hearsay,
Sought for their kith and their kin among the few-acred farmers
On the Acadian coast, and the prairies of fair Opelousas.
With them Evageline went, and her guide, the Father Felician.
Onward o'er sunken sands, through a wilderness sombre with forests,
Day after day they glided adown the turbulent river;
Night after night, by their blazing fires, encamped on its borders.
Now through rushing chutes, among green islands, where plumelike
Cotton-trees nodded their shadowy crests, they swept with the current,
Then emerged into broad lagoons, where silvery sand-bars

Lay in the stream, and along the wimpling waves of their margin,
Shining with snow-white plumes, large flocks of pelicans waded.
Level the landscape grew, and along the shores of the river,
Shaded by China-trees, in the midst of luxuriant gardens,
Stood the houses of planters, with negro-cabins and dove-cots.
They were approaching the region where reigns perpetual summer,
Where through the Golden Coast, and groves of orange and citron,
Sweeps with majestic curve the river away to the eastward.
They, too, swerved from their course; and, entering the Bayou of Plaquemine,
Soon were lost in a maze of sluggish and devious waters,
Which, like a network of steel, extended in every direction.
Over their heads the towering and tenebrous boughs of the cypress
Met in a dusky arch, and trailing mosses in mid-air
Waved like banners that hang on the walls of ancient cathedrals.
Deathlike the silence seemed, and unbroken, save by the herons
Home to their roosts in the cedar-trees returning at sunset,
Or by the owl, as he greeted the moon with demoniac laughter.
Lovely the moonlight was as it glanced and gleamed on the water,
Gleamed on the columns of cypress and cedar sustaining the arches,

Down through whose broken vaults it fell as through
chinks in a ruin.
Dreamlike, and indistinct, and strange were all things
around them;
And o'er their spirits there came a feeling of wonder
and sadness,—
Strange forebodings of ill, unseen and that cannot be
compassed.
As, at the tramp of a horse's hoof on the turf of the
prairies,
Far in advance are closed the leaves of the shrinking
mimosa,
So, at the hoof-beats of fate, with sad forebodings of
evil,
Shrinks and closes the heart, ere the stroke of doom has
attained it.
But Evangeline's heart was sustained by a vision, that
faintly
Floated before her eyes, and beckoned her on through
the moonlight.
It was the thought of her brain that assumed the shape
of a phantom.
Through those shadowy aisles had Gabriel wandered
before her,
And every stroke of the oar now brought him nearer
and nearer.

Then in his place, at the prow of the boat, rose one of
the oarsmen,
And, as a signal sound, if others like them perad-
venture
Sailed on those gloomy and midnight streams, blew a
blast on his bugle.
Wild through the dark colonnades and corridors leafy
the blast rang,
Breaking the seal of silence, and giving tongues to the
forest.

Soundless above them the banners of moss just stirred
to the music.
Multitudinous echoes awoke and died in the distance,
Over the watery floor, and beneath the reverberant
branches;
But not a voice replied; no answer came from the
darkness;
And when the echoes had ceased, like a sense of pain
was the silence.
Then Evangeline slept; but the boatmen rowed through
the midnight,
Silent at times, then singing familiar Canadian boat-
songs,
Such as they sang of old on their own Acadian river,
While through the night were heard the mysterious
sounds of the desert,
Far off,—indistinct,— as of wave or wind in the forest,
Mixed with the whoop of the crane and the roar of the
grim alligator.

Thus ere another noon they emerged from the
shades; and before them
Lay, in the golden sun, the lakes of the Atchafalaya.
Water-lilies in myriads rocked on the slight undulations
Made by the passing oars, and, resplendent in beauty,
the lotus
Lifted her golden crown above the heads of the
boatmen.
Faint was the air with the odorous breath of magnolia
blossoms,
And with the heat of noon; and numberless sylvan
islands,
Fragrant and thickly embowered with blossoming
hedges of roses,
Near to whose shores they glided along, invited to
slumber.

Soon by the fairest of these their weary oars were suspended.
Under the boughs of Wachita willows, that grew by the margin,
Safely their boat was moored; and scattered about on the greensward,
Tired with their midnight toil, the weary travellers slumbered.
Over them vast and high extended the cope of a cedar.
Swinging from its great arms, the trumpet-flower and the grape-vine
Hung their ladders of rope aloft like the ladder of Jacob,
On whose pendulous stairs the angels ascending, descending,
Were the swift humming-birds, that flitted from blossom to blossom.
Such was the vision Evangeline saw as she slumbered beneath it.
Filled was her heart with love, and the dawn of an opening heaven
Lighted her soul in sleep with the glory of regions celestial.

Nearer and ever nearer, among the numberless islands,
Darted a light, swift boat, that sped away o'er the water,
Urged on its course by the sinewy arms of hunters and trappers.
Northward its prow was turned, to the land of the bison and beaver.
At the helm sat a youth, with countenance thoughtful and careworn.
Dark and neglected locks overshadowed his brow, and a sadness

Somewhat beyond his years on his face was legibly written.
Gabriel was it, who, weary with waiting, unhappy and restless,
All undisturbed by the dash of their oars, and of sorrow.
Swiftly they glided along, close under the lee of the island,
But by the opposite bank, and behind a screen of palmettos,
So that they saw not the boat, where it lay concealed in the willows,
All undisturbed by the dash of their oars, and unseen, were the sleepers,
Angel of God was there none to awaken the slumbering maiden.
Swiftly they glided away, like the shade of a cloud on the prairie.
After the sound of their oars on the tholes had died in the distance,
As from a magic trance the sleepers awoke, and the maiden
Said with a sigh to the friendly priest, "O Father Felician!
Something says in my heart that near me Gabriel wanders.
Is it a foolish dream, an idle and vague superstition?
Or has an angel passed, and revealed the truth to my spirit?"
Then, with a blush, she added,—"Alas for my credulous fancy!
Unto ears like thine such words as these have no meaning."
But made answer the reverend man, and he smiled as he answered,—
"Daughter, thy words are not idle; nor are they to me without meaning.
Feeling is deep and still; and the word that floats on the surface

Is as the tossing buoy, that betrays where the anchor is hidden.
Therefore trust to thy heart, and to what the world calls illusions.
Gabriel truly is near thee; for not far away to the southward,
On the banks of the Têche are the towns of St. Maur and St. Martin.
There the long-wandering bride shall be given again to her bridegroom,
There the long-absent pastor regain his flock and his sheepfold.
Beautiful is the land, with its prairies and forests of fruit-trees;
Under the feet a garden of flowers, and the bluest of heavens
Bending above, and resting its dome on the walls of the forest.
They who dwell there have named it the Eden of Louisiana."
With their words of cheer they arose and continued on their journey.
Softly the evening came. The sun from the western horizon
Like a magician extended his golden wand o'er the landscape;
Twinkling vapours arose; and sky and water and forest
Seemed all on fire at the touch, and melted and mingled together.
Hanging between two skies, a cloud with edges of silver,
Floated the boat, with its dripping oars, on the motionless water.
Filled was Evangeline's heart with inexpressible sweetness.
Touched by the magic spell, the sacred fountains of feeling

Glowed with the light of love, as the skies and waters around her.
Then from a neighbouring thicket the mockingbird, wildest of singers,
Swinging aloft on a willow spray that hung o'er the water,
Shook from his little throat such floods of delirious music,
That the whole air and the woods and the waves seemed silent to listen.
Plaintive at first were the tones and sad: then soaring to madness
Seemed they to follow or guide the revel of frenzied Bacchantes.
Single notes were then heard, in sorrowful, low lamentation;
Till, having gathered them all, he flung them abroad in derision,
As when, after a storm, a gust of wind through the tree-tops
Shakes down the rattling rain in a crystal shower on the branches.
With such a prelude as this, and hearts that throbbed with emotion,
Slowly they entered the Têche, where it flows through the green Opelousas,
And through the amber air, above the crest of the woodland,
Saw the column of smoke that arose from a neighbouring dwelling;—
Sounds of a horn they heard, and the distant lowing of cattle.

III

Near to the bank of the river, o're-shadowed by oaks, from whose branches

Garlands of Spanish moss and of mystic mistletoe flaunted,
Such as the Druids cut down with golden hatchets at Yuletide,
Stood, secluded and still, the house of the herdsman. A garden
Girded it round about with a belt of luxuriant blossoms,
Filling the air with fragrance. The house itself was of timbers
Hewn from the cypress-tree, and carefully fitted together.
Large and low was the roof; and on slender columns supported,
Rose-wreathed, vine-encircled, a broad and spacious veranda,
Haunt of the humming-bird and the bee, extended around it.
At each end of the house, amid the flowers of the garden,
Stationed the dove-cots were, as love's perpetual symbol,
Scenes of endless wooing, and endless contentions of rivals.
Silence reigned o'er the place. The line of shadow and sunshine
Ran near the tops of the trees; but the house itself was in shadow,
And from its chimney-top, ascending and slowly expanding
Into the evening air, a thin blue column of smoke rose.
In the rear of the house, from the garden gate, ran a pathway
Through the great groves of oak to the skirts of the limitless prairie,
Into whose sea of flowers the sun was slowly descending.
Full in his track of light, like ships with shadowy canvas

Hanging loose from their spars in a motionless calm in the tropics,
Stood a cluster of trees, with tangled cordage of grape-vines.

Just where the woodlands met the flowery surf of the prairie,
Mounted upon his horse, with Spanish saddle and stirrups,
Sat a herdsman, arrayed in gaiters and doublet of deerskin.
Broad and brown was the face that from under the Spanish sombrero
Gazed on the peaceful scene, with the lordly look of its master.
Round about him were numberless herds of kine, that were grazing
Quietly in the meadows, and breathing the vapoury freshness
That uprose from the river, and spread itself over the landscape.
Slowly lifting the horn that hung at his side, and expanding
Fully his broad, deep chest, he blew a blast, that resounded
Wildly and sweet and far, through the still damp air of the evening.
Suddenly out of the grass the long white horns of the cattle
Rose like flakes of foam on the adverse currents of ocean.
Silent a moment they gazed, then bellowing rushed o'er the prairie,
And the whole mass became a cloud, a shade in the distance.
Then, as the herdsman turned to the house, through the gate of the garden

Saw he the forms of the priest and the maiden
advancing to meet him.
Suddenly down from his horse he sprang in amazement,
and forward
Rushed with extended arms and exclamations of
wonder;
When they beheld his face, they recognized Basil, the
blacksmith.
Hearty his welcome was, as he led his guests to the
garden.
There in an arbour of roses with endless question and
answer
Gave they vent to their hearts, and renewed their
friendly embraces.
Laughing and weeping by turns, or sitting silent and
thoughtful.
Thoughtful, for Gabriel came not; and now dark doubts
and misgivings
Stole o'er the maiden's heart; and Basil, somewhat
embarrassed,
Broke the silence and said,—"If you came by the
Atchafalaya,
How have you nowhere encountered my Gabriel's boat
on the bayous?"
Over Evangeline's face at the words of Basil a shade
passed.
Tears came into her eyes, and she said, with a tremulous
accent,
"Gone? is Gabriel gone?" and, concealing her face on
his shoulder,
All her o'erburdened heart gave way, and she wept and
lamented.
Then the good Basil said,—and his voice grew blithe as
he said it,—
"Be of good cheer, my child; it is only to-day he
departed.
Foolish boy! he has left me alone with my herds and my
horses.

Moody and restless grown, and tried and troubled, his spirit
Could no longer endure the calm of this quiet existence,
Thinking ever of thee, uncertain and sorrowful ever,
Ever silent, or speaking only of thee and his troubles,
He at length had become so tedious to men and to maidens,
Tedious even to me, that at length I bethought me, and sent him
Unto the town of Adayes to trade for mules with the Spaniards.
Thence he will follow the Indian trails to the Ozark Mountains,
Hunting for furs in the forests, on rivers trapping the beaver.
Therefore be of good cheer; we will follow the fugitive lover;
He is not far on his way, and the Fates and the streams are against him.
Up and away to-morrow, and through the red dew of the morning
We will follow him fast, and bring him back to his prison."
Then glad voices were heard, and up from the banks of the river,
Borne aloft on his comrades' arms, came Michael the fiddler.
Long under Basil's roof had he lived like a god on Olympus,
Having no other care than dispensing music to mortals.
Far renowned was he for his silver locks and his fiddle.
"Long live Michael!" they cried, "our brave Acadian minstrel!"
As they bore him aloft in triumphal procession; and straightway
Father Felician advanced with Evangeline, greeting the old man

Kindly and oft, and recalling the past, while Basil, enraptured,
Hailed with hilarious joy his old companions and gossips,
Laughing loud and long, and embracing mothers and daughters.
Much they marvelled to see the wealth of the ci-devant blacksmith,
All his domains and his herds, and his patriarchal demeanour;
Much they marvelled to hear his tales of the soil and the climate,
And of the prairies, whose numberless herds were his who would take them;
Each one thought in his heart, that he, too, would go and do likewise.
Thus they ascended the steps, and, crossing the breezy veranda,
Entered the hall of the house, where already the supper of Basil
Waited his late return; and they rested and feasted together.

Over the joyous feast the sudden darkness descended.
All was silent without, and illuming the landscape with silver,
Fair rose the dewy moon and the myriad stars; but within doors,
Brighter than these, shone the faces of friends in the glimmering lamplight.
Then from his station aloft, at the head of the table, the herdsman
Poured forth his heart and his wine together in endless profusion.
Lighting his pipe, that was filled with sweet Natchitoches tobacco,

Thus he spake to his guests, who listened, and smiled as they listened:—
"Welcome once more, my friends, who long have been friendless and homeless,
Welcome once more to a home, that is better perchance than the old one!
Here no hungry winter congeals our blood like the rivers;
Here no stony ground provokes the wrath of the farmer.
Smoothly the ploughshare runs through the soil, as a keel through the water.
All the year round the orange-groves are in blossom; and grass grows
More in a single night than a whole Canadian summer.
Here, too, numberless herds run wild and unclaimed in the prairies;
Here, too, lands may be had for the asking, and forests of timber
With a few blows of the axe are hewn and framed into houses.
After your houses are built, and your fields are yellow with harvests,
No King George of England shall drive you away from your homesteads,
Burning your dwellings and barns, and stealing your farms and your cattle."
Speaking these words, he blew a wrathful cloud from his nostrils,
While his huge, brown hand came thundering down on the table,
So that the guests all started; and Father Felician astounded,
Suddenly paused, with a pinch of snuff half-way to his nostrils.
But the brave Basil resumed, and his words were milder and gayer:—
"Only beware of the fever, my friends, beware of the fever!

For it is not like that of our cold Acadian climate,
Cured by wearing a spider hung round one's neck in a nutshell!"
Then there were voices heard at the door, and footsteps approaching
Sounded upon the stairs and the floor of the breezy verandah.
It was the neighbouring Creoles and small Acadian planters,
Who had been summoned all to the house of Basil the herdsman.
Merry the meeting was of ancient comrades and neighbours:
Friend clasped friend in his arms; and they who before were strangers,
Meeting in exile, came straightway as friends to each other,
Drawn by the gentle bond of a common country together.
But in the neighbouring hall a strain of music, proceeding
From the accordant strings of Michael's melodious fiddle,
Broke up all further speech. Away, like children delighted,
All things forgotten beside, they gave themselves to the maddening
Whirl of the giddy dance, as it swept and swayed to the music,
Dreamlike, with beaming eyes and the rush of fluttering garments.

Meanwhile, apart at the head of the hall, the priest and the herdsman
Sat, conversing together of past and present and future;
While Evangeline stood like one entranced, for within her

Olden memories rose, and loud in the midst of the music
Heard she the sound of the sea, and an irrepresible sadness
Came o'er her heart, and unseen she stole forth into the garden.
Beautiful was the night. Behind the black wall of the forests,
Tipping its summit with silver, arose the moon. On the river
Fell here and there through the branches a tremulous gleam of the moonlight,
Like the sweet thoughts of love on a darkened and devious spirit.
Nearer and round about her, the manifold flowers of the garden
Poured out their souls in odours, that were their prayers and confessions
Unto the night, as it went its way, like a silent Carthusian.
Fuller of fragrance than they, and as heavy with shadows and night-dews,
Hung the heart of the maiden. The calm and the magical moonlight
Seemed to inundate her soul with indefinable longings,
As, through the garden gate, and beneath the brown shade of the oak-trees,
Passed she along the path to the edge of the measureless prairie.
Silent it lay, with a silvery haze upon it, and fireflies
Gleamed and floated away in mingled and infinite numbers.
Over her head the stars, the thoughts of God in the heavens,
Shone on the eyes of man, who had ceased to marvel and worship,
Save when a blazing comet was seen on the walls of that temple,

As if a hand had appeared and written upon them, "Upharsin."
And the soul of the maiden, between the stars and the fire-flies,
Wandered alone, and she cried,—"O Gabriel! O my beloved!
Art thou so near unto me, and yet I cannot behold thee?
Art thou so near unto me, and yet thy voice does not reach me?
Ah! how often thy feet have trod this path to the prairie!
Ah! how often thine eyes have looked on the woodlands around me!
Ah! how often beneath this oak, returning from labour,
Thou hast lain down to rest, and to dream of me in thy slumbers!
When shall these eyes behold, these arms be folded about thee?"
Loud and sudden and near the notes of a whippoorwill sounded
Like a flute in the woods; and anon, through the neighbouring thickets,
Farther and farther away it floated and dropped into silence.
"Patience!" whispered the oaks from oracular caverns of darkness:
And, from the moonlit meadow, a sigh responded, "To-morrow!"

Bright rose the sun next day; and all the flowers of the garden
Bathed his shining feet with their tears, and anointed his tresses
With the delicious balm that they bore in their vases of crystal.
"Farewell!" said the priest, as he stood at the shadowy threshold;

"See that you bring us the Prodigal Son from his fasting and famine;
And, too, the Foolish Virgin, who slept when the bridegroom was coming."
"Farewell!" answered the maiden, and, smiling, with Basil descended
Down to the river's brink, where the boatmen already were waiting.
Thus beginning their journey with morning, and sunshine, and gladness,
Swiftly they followed the flight of him who was speeding before them,
Blown by the blast of fate like a dead leaf over the desert.
Not that day, nor the next, nor yet the day that succeeded,
Found they the trace of his course, in lake or forest or river,
Nor, after many days, had they found him; but vague and uncertain
Rumours alone were their guides through a wild and desolate country;
Till, at the little inn of the Spanish town of Adayes,
Weary and worn, they alighted, and learned from the garrulous landlord,
That on the day before, with horses and guides and companions,
Gabriel left the village, and took the road of the prairies.

IV

Far in the West there lies a desert land, where the mountains
Lift, through perpetual snows, their lofty and luminous summits.

Down from their jagged, deep ravines, where the gorge, like a gateway,
Opens a passage rude to the wheels of the emigrant's wagon,
Westward the Oregon flows and the Walleway and Owyhee.
Eastward, with devious course, among the Windriver mountains,
Through the Sweet-water Valley precipitate leaps the Nebraska;
And to the south, from Fontaine-qui-bout and the Spanish sierras,
Fretted with sands and rocks, and swept by the wind of the desert,
Numberless torrents, with ceaseless sound, descend to the ocean,
Like the great chords of a harp, in loud and solemn vibrations.
Spreading between these streams are the wondrous, beautiful prairies;
Billowy bays of grass ever rolling in shadow and sunshine,
Bright with luxuriant clusters of roses and purple amorphas.
Over them wandered the buffalo herds, and the elk and the roebuck;
Over them wandered the wolves, and herds of riderless horses;
Fires that blast and blight, and winds that are weary with travel;
Over them wander the scattered tribes of Ishmael's children,
Staining the desert with blood; and above their terrible war-trails
Circles and sails aloft, on pinions majestic, the vulture,
Like the implacable soul of a chieftain slaughtered in battle,

By invisible stairs ascending and scaling the heavens.
Here and there rise smokes from the camps of these savage marauders;
Here and there rise groves from the margins of swift-running rivers;
And the grim, taciturn bear, the anchorite monk of the desert,
Climbs down their dark ravines to dig for roots by the brookside;
And over all is the sky, the clear and crystalline heaven,
Like the protecting hand of God inverted above them.

Into this wonderful land, at the base of the Ozark Mountains,
Gabriel far had entered, with hunters and trappers behind him.
Day after day, with their Indian guides, the maiden and Basil
Followed his flying steps, and thought each day to o'ertake him.
Sometimes they saw, or thought they saw, the smoke of his camp-fire
Rise in the morning air from the distant plain; but at nightfall,
When they had reached the place, they found only embers and ashes.
And, though their hearts were sad at times and their bodies were weary,
Hope still guided them on, as the magic Fata Morgana
Showed them her lakes of light, that retreated and vanished before them.

Once, as they sat by their evening fire, there silently entered
Into their little camp an Indian woman, whose features

Wore deep traces of sorrow, and patience as great as her sorrow.
She was a Shawnee woman returning home to her people,
From the far-off hunting grounds of the cruel Camanches,
Where her Canadian husband, a Coureur-de-Bois, had been murdered.
Touched were their hearts at her story, and warmest and friendliest welcome
Gave they, with words of cheer, and she sat and feasted among them
On the buffalo meat and the venison cooked on the embers.
But when their meal was done, and Basil and all his companions,
Worn with the long day's march and the chase of the deer and the bison,
Stretched themselves on the ground, and slept where the quivering fire-light
Flashed on their swarthy cheeks, and their forms wrapped up in their blankets,
Then at the door of Evangeline's tent she sat and repeated
Slowly, with soft, low voice, and the charm of her Indian accent,
All the tale of her love, with its pleasures, and pains, and reverses.
Much Evangeline wept at the tale, and to know that another
Hapless heart like her own had loved and had been disappointed.
Moved to the depths of her soul by pity and woman's compassion,
Yet in her sorrow pleased that one who had suffered was near her,
She in turn related her love and all its disasters.

Mute with wonder the Shawnee sat, and when she had ended
Still was mute; but at length, as if a mysterious horror
Passed through her brain, she spake, and repeated the tale of the Mowis;
Mowis, he bridegroom of snow, who won and wedded a maiden,
But, when the morning came, arose and passed from the wigwam,
Fading and melting away and dissolving into the sunshine,
Till she beheld him no more, though she followed far into the forest.
Then, in those sweet, low tones, that seemed like a weird incantation,
Told she the tale of the fair Lilinau, who was wooed by a phantom,
That, through the pines, o'er her father's lodge, in the hush of the twilight,
Breathed like the evening wind, and whispered love to the maiden,
Till she followed his green and waving plume through the forest,
And nevermore returned, nor was seen again by her people.
Silent with wonder and strange surprise, Evangeline listened
To the soft flow of her magical words, till the region around her
Seemed like enchanted ground, and her swarthy guest the enchantress.
Slowly over the tops of the Ozark Mountains the moon rose,
Lighting the little tent, and with a mysterious splendour
Touching the sombre leaves, and embracing and filling the woodland.
With a delicate sound the brook rushed by, and the branches.

Swayed and sighed overhead in scarcely audible
whispers.
Filled with the thoughts of love was Evangeline's heart,
but a secret,
Subtle sense crept in of pain and indefinte terror,
As the cold poisonous snake creeps into the nest of the
swallow.
It was no earthly fear. A breath from the region of
spirits
Seemed to float in the air of night; and she felt for a
moment
That, like the Indian maid, she, too, was pursuing a
phantom.
With this thought she slept, and the fear and the
phantom had vanished.

Early upon the morrow the march was resumed; and
the Shawnee
Said, as they journeyed along,—"On the western slope
of these mountains
Dwells in his little village the Black Robe chief of the
Mission.
Much he teaches the people, and tells them of Mary and
Jesus;
Loud laugh their hearts with joy, and weep with pain,
as they hear him."
Then, with a sudden and secret emotion, Evangeline
answered,—
"Let us go to the Mission, for there good tidings await
us!"
Thither they turned their steeds; and behind a spur of
the mountains,
Just as the sun went down, they heard a murmur of
voices,
And in a meadow green and broad, by the bank of a
river,

Saw the tents of the Christians, the tents of the Jesuit Mission.
Under a towering oak, that stood in the midst of the village,
Knelt the Black Robe chief with his children. A crucifix fastened
High on the trunk of the tree, and over-shadowed by grape-vines,
Looked with its agonised face on the multitude kneeling beneath it.
This was their rural chapel. Aloft, through the intricate arches
Of its aerial roof, arose the chant of their vespers,
Mingling its notes with the soft susurrus and sighs of the branches.
Silent, with heads uncovered, the travellers, nearer approaching,
Knelt on the swarded floor, and joined in the evening devotions.
But when the service was done, and the benediction had fallen
Forth from the hands of the priest, like seed from the hands of the sower,
Slowly the reverend man advanced to the strangers, and bade them
Welcome; and when they replied, he smiled with benignant expression,
Hearing the homelike sounds of his mother-tongue in the forest,
And, with words of kindness, conducted them into his wigwam.
There upon mats and skins they reposed, and on cakes of the maize-ear
Feasted, and slaked their thirst from the water-gourd of the teacher.
Soon was their story told; and the priest with solemnity answered:—

"Not six suns have risen and set since Gabriel, seated
On this mat by my side, where now the maiden reposes,
Told me this same sad tale; then arose and continued his journey!"
Soft was the voice of the priest, and he spake with an accent of kindness;
But on Evangeline's heart fell his words as in winter the snow-flakes
Fall into some lone nest from which the birds have departed.
"Far to the north he has gone," continued the priest; "but in autumn,
When the chase is done, will return again to the Mission."
Then Evangeline said, and her voice was meek and submissive,
"Let me remain with thee, for my soul is sad and afflicted."
So seemed it wise and well unto all; and betimes on the morrow,
Mounting his Mexican steed, with his Indian guides and companions,
Homeward Basil returned, and Evangeline stayed at the Mission.

Slowly, slowly, slowly the days succeeded each other,—
Days and weeks and months; and the fields of maize that were springing
Green from the ground when a stranger she came, now waving above her,
Lifted their slender shafts, with leaves interlacing, and forming
Cloisters for mendicant crows and granaries pillaged by squirrels.
Then in the golden weather the maize was husked, and the maidens

Blushed at each blood-red ear, for that betokened a lover,
But at the crooked laughed, and called it a thief in the corn-field.
Even the blood-red ear to Evangeline brought not her lover.
"Patience!" the priest would say; "Have faith, and thy prayer will be answered!
Look at this vigorous plant that lifts its head from the meadow,
See how its leaves are turned to the north, as true as the magnet;
This is the compass flower, that the finger of God has planted
Here in the houseless wild, to direct the traveller's journey
Over the sea-like, pathless, limitless waste of the desert.
Such in the soul of man is faith. The blossoms of passion,
Gay and luxuriant flowers, are brighter and fuller of fragrance,
But they beguile us, and lead us astray, and their odour is deadly.
Only this humble plant can guide us here, and hereafter
Crown us with asphodel flowers, that are wet with the dews of nepenthe."

So came the autumn, and passed, and the winter,—yet Gabriel came not;
Blossomed the opening spring, and the notes of the robin and blue-bird
Sounded sweet upon wold and in wood, yet Gabriel came not.
But on the breath of the summer winds a rumor was wafted
Sweeter than song of bird, or hue or odour of blossom.

Far to the north and east, it said, in the Michigan forests,
Gabriel had his lodge by the banks of the Saginaw River.
And, with returning guides, that sought the lakes of St. Lawrence,
Saying a sad farewell, Evangeline went from the Mission.
When over weary ways, by long and perilous marches,
She had attained at length the depths of the Michigan forests,
Found she the hunter's lodge deserted and fallen to ruin!

Thus did the long sad years glide on, and in seasons and places
Divers and distant far was seen the wandering maiden;—
Now in the Tents of Grace of the meek Moravian Missions,
Now in the noisy camps and the battlefields of the army,
Now in secluded hamlets, in towns and populous cities.
Like a phantom she came, and passed away unremembered.
Fair was she and young, when in hope began the long journey;
Faded was she and old, when in disappointment it ended.
Each succeeding year stole something away from her beauty,
Leaving behind it, broader and deeper, the gloom and the shadow.
Then there appeared and spread faint streaks of gray o'er her forehead,
Dawn of another life, that broke o'er her earthly horizon,

As in the eastern sky the first faint streaks of the morning.

V

In that delightful land which is washed by the Delaware waters,
Guarding in sylvan shades the name of Penn the apostle,
Stands on the banks of its beautiful stream the city he founded.
There all the air is balm, and the peach is the emblem of beauty,
And the streets still re-echo the names of the trees of the forest,
As if they fain would appease the Dryads whose haunts they molested.
There from the troubled sea had Evangeline landed, an exile,
Finding among the children of Penn a home and a country.
There old René Leblanc had died; and when he departed,
Saw at his side only one of all his hundred descendants.
Something at least there was in the friendly streets of the city,
Something that spake to her heart, and made her no longer a stranger;
And her ear was pleased with the Thee and Thou of the Quakers,
For it recalled the past, the old Acadian country,
Where all men were equal, and all were brothers and sisters.
So, when the fruitless search, the disappointed endeavour,
Ended, to recommence no more upon earth, uncomplaining,

Thither, as leaves the light, were turned her thoughts and her footsteps.
As from a mountain's top the rainy mists of the morning
Roll away, and afar we behold the landscape below us,
Sun-illumined, with shining rivers and cities and hamlets,
So fell the mists from her mind, and she saw the world far below her,
Dark no longer, but illumined with love; and the pathway
Which she had climbed so far, lying smooth and fair in the distance,
Gabriel was not forgotten. Within her heart was his image,
Clothed in the beauty of love and youth, as last she beheld him,
Only more beautiful made by his deathlike silence and absence.
Into her thoughts of him time entered not, for it was not.
Over him years had no power; he was not changed, but transfigured;
He had become to her heart as one who is dead, and not absent;
Patience and abnegation of self, and devotion to others,
This was the lesson a life of trial and sorrow had taught her.
So was her love diffused, but, like to some odorous spices,
Suffered no waste nor loss, though filling the air with aroma.
Other hope had she none, nor wish in life, but to follow
Meekly, with reverent steps, the sacred feet of her Saviour.
Thus many years she lived as a Sister of Mercy; frequenting

Lonely and wretched roofs in the crowded lanes of the city,
Where distress and want concealed themselves from the sunlight,
Where disease and sorrow in garrets languished neglected.
Night after night, when the world was asleep, as the watchman repeated
Loud, through the gusty streets, that all was well in the city,
High at some lonely window he saw the light of her taper.
Day after day, in the gray of the dawn, as slow through the suburbs
Plodded the German farmer, with flowers and fruits for the market,
Met he that meek, pale face, returning home from its watchings.

Then it came to pass that a pestilence fell on the city,
Presaged by wondrous signs, and mostly by flocks of wild pigeons,
Darkening the sun in their flight, with naught in their craws but an acorn.
And, as the tides of the sea arise in the mouth of September,
Flooding some silver stream, till it spreads to a lake in the meadow,
So death flooded life, and o'erflowing its natural margin,
Spread to a brackish lake, the silver stream of existence.
Wealth had no power to bribe, nor beauty to charm, the oppressor;
But all perished alike beneath the scourge of his anger;—
Only, alas! the poor, who had neither friends nor attendants,

Crept away to die in the almshouse, home of the homeless.
Then in the suburbs it stood, in the midst of meadows and woodlands;—
Now the city surrounds it; but still, with its gateway and wicket
Meek, in the midst of splendour, its humble walls seem to echo
Softly the words of the Lord:—"The poor ye always have with you."
Thither, by night and by day, came the Sister of Mercy. The dying
Looked up into her face, and thought, indeed, to behold there
Gleams of celestial light encircle her forehead with splendour,
Such as the artist paints o'er the brows of saints and apostles,
Or such as hangs by night o'er a city seen at a distance.
Unto their eyes it seemed the lamps of the city celestial,
Into whose shining gates ere long their spirits would enter.

Thus, on a Sabbath morn, through the streets, deserted and silent,
Wending her quiet way, she entered the door of the almshouse.
Sweet on the summer air was the odour of flowers in the garden;
And she paused on her way to gather the fairest among them,
That the dying once more might rejoice in their fragrance and beauty.
Then, as she mounted the stairs to the corridors, cooled by the east-wind,

Distant and soft on her ear fell the chimes from the belfry of Christ Church,
While, intermingled with these, across the meadows were wafted
Sounds of psalms, that were sung by the Swedes in their church at Wicaco.
Soft as descending wings fell the calm of the hour on her spirit:
Something within her said,—"At length thy trials are ended;"
And, with light in her looks, she entered the chambers of sickness.
Noiselessly moved about the assiduous careful attendants,
Moistening the feverish lip, and the aching brow, and in silence
Closing the sightless eyes of the dead, and concealing their faces,
Where on their pallets they lay, like drifts of snow by the roadside.
Many a languid head, upraised as Evangeline entered,
Turned on its pillow of pain to gaze while she passed, for her presence
Fell on their hearts like a ray of the sun on the walls of a prison.
And, as she looked around, she saw how Death, the consoler,
Laying his hand upon many a heart, had healed it for ever.
Many familiar forms had disappeared in the night time;
Vacant their places were, or filled already by strangers.

Suddenly, as if arrested by fear or a feeling of wonder,
Still she stood, with her colourless lips apart, while a shudder

Ran through her frame, and, forgotten, the flowerets dropped from her fingers,
And from her eyes and cheeks the light and bloom of the morning.
Then there escaped from her lips a cry of such terrible anguish,
That the dying heard it, and started up from their pillows.
On the pallet before her was stretched the form of an old man.
Long, and thin, and gray were the locks that shaded his temples;
But, as he lay in the morning light, his face for a moment
Seemed to assume once more the forms of its earlier manhood;
So are wont to be changed the faces of those who are dying.
Hot and red on his lips still burned the flush of the fever,
As if life, like the Hebrew, with blood had besprinkled its portals,
That the Angel of Death might see the sign, and pass over.
Motionless, senseless, dying, he lay, and his spirit exhausted
Seemed to be sinking down through infinite depths in the darkness,
Darkness of slumber and death, forever sinking and sinking.
Then through those realms of shade, in multiplied reverberations,
Heard he that cry of pain, and through the hush that succeeded
Whispered a gentle voice, in accents tender and saint-like,
"Gabriel! O my beloved!" and died away into silence.

Then he beheld, in a dream, once more the home of his childhood;
Green Acadian meadows, with sylvan rivers among them,
Village, and mountain, and woodlands; and, walking under their shadow,
As in the days of her youth, Evangeline rose in his vision.
Tears came into his eyes; and as slowly he lifted his eyelids,
Vanished the vision away, but Evangeline knelt by his bedside.
Vainly he strove to whisper her name, for the accents unuttered
Died on his lips, and their motion revealed what his tongue would have spoken.
Vainly he strove to rise; and Evangeline, kneeling beside him,
Kissed his dying lips, and laid his head on her bosom.
Sweet was the light of his eyes; but it suddenly sank into darkness,
As when a lamp is blown out by a gust of wind at a casement.

All was ended now, the hope, and the fear, and the sorrow,
All the aching of heart, the restless, unsatisfied longing,
All the dull, deep pain, and constant anguish of patience!
And, as she pressed once more the lifeless head to her bosom,
Meekly she bowed her own, and muttered, "Father, I thank Thee!"

Still stands the forests primeval; but far away from its shadow,

Side by side, in their nameless graves, the lovers are sleeping.
Under the humble walls of the little Catholic church yard,
In the heart of the city, they lie, unknown and unnoticed.
Daily the tides of life go ebbing and flowing beside them,
Thousands of throbbing hearts, where theirs are at rest and forever,
Thousands of aching brains, where theirs no longer are busy,
Thousands of toiling hands, where theirs have ceased from their labours,
Thousands of weary feet, where theirs have completed their journey!

Still stands the forest primeval; but under the shade of its branches
Dwells another race, with other customs and language.
Only along the shore of the mournful and misty Atlantic
Linger a few Acadian peasants, whose fathers from exile
Wandered back to their native land to die in its bosom.
In the fisherman's cot the wheel and the loom are still busy;
Maidens still wear their Norman caps and their kirtles of homespun,
And by the evening fire repeat Evangeline's story,
While from its rocky caverns the deep-voiced, neighbouring ocean
Speaks, and in accents disconsolate answers the wail of the forest.